ACT LIKE MEN—BE STRONG

ACT LIKE MEN
BE STRONG

How to Develop Biblical Manhood

JIM GRASSI, D.MIN.

Foreword by
KEN HARRISON,
Chairman of the Board, Promise Keepers

ACT LIKE MEN – BE STRONG
How to Develop Biblical Manhood

Promise Keepers Publications: Colorado Springs, Colorado

DEDICATION

To men of promise who aspire to know God and make Him known—
men who dare to be great and compassionate warriors for their families,
churches, communities, and nation.

For the Lord is good and His love endures forever;
His faithfulness continues through all generations.
— Psalm 100:5

My people, hear my teaching;
listen to the words of my mouth.
I will open my mouth with a parable;
I will utter hidden things, things from of old—
things we have heard and known,
things our ancestors have told us.

We will not hide them from their descendants;
we will tell the next generation
the praiseworthy deeds of the Lord,
his power, and the wonders he has done.
He decreed statutes for Jacob
and established the law in Israel,
which he commanded our ancestors
to teach their children,
so the next generation would know them,
even the children yet to be born,
and they in turn would tell their children.

Then they would put their trust in God
and would not forget his deeds
but would keep his commands.
They would not be like their ancestors—
a stubborn and rebellious generation,
whose hearts were not loyal to God,
whose spirits were not faithful to him.
– Psalm 78:1-8

TABLE OF CONTENTS

ACKNOWLEDGMENTS

I praise God for the many relationships, experiences, and wisdom He has given me to formulate the concepts within this work. When Jesus said, "Follow Me, and I will make you fishers of men" (Matt. 4:19), He started a revival of spirit and hope that changed the world. Shortly thereafter, men began to gather together for worship and fellowship.

Isn't it interesting that when Jesus started His ministry, He picked eight fishermen to be among the initial twelve disciples? He knew that the same passion, zeal, and perseverance that inspired His fishermen to be successful in catching fish would now be utilized to catch men, women, boys, and girls who would follow His Word. Our Lord's inspiration to His disciples helped them see the importance of knowing God and making Him known. If twelve common men could impact the world for Christ's sake, what can we do with the power of the Holy Spirit and the many resources available to us today? The power of His Word cannot be denied.

In my study of Scripture, there are five places that helped me better understand the importance of what godly manhood means and how to be His disciple (spiritual mentor): 1 Corinthians 16:13-14, Matthew 28, Matthew 4:17–20, Romans 12 and Titus 2. In this work, I have discussed how each of these timely scriptures helped shape my perspective and mission when it comes to living out my faith and understanding what biblical manhood looks like.

As our Lord began His teaching, He challenged His followers with these words: "The time is fulfilled, and the Kingdom of God is at hand. Repent, and believe in the gospel" (Mark 1:15 NKJV). Certainly, the fulfilling of biblical prophecy suggests that, for believers, the kingdom of heaven is nearer today than it was at the time of Christ. Are you ready for His return? I hope you are and that this work might help you better live out a believer's role and challenge during the end-times.

I greatly appreciate the patience and grace given to me by my wonderful wife, Louise, and by our talented Men's Ministry Catalyst team. I'm especially indebted to all our ministry partners, supporters, and board members who have faithfully served and supported our ministry and me during the past four decades of serving our Lord.

The contributions and encouragement I've received from friends like Ken Harrison, Judge Vance Day, Rob Fischer, Dr. John Denney, Dr. Michael Gurian, Dr. Karen C. Johnson, Jeff Klippenes, Peter Menconi, Dr. Chuck Stecker, Dr. Chuck Swindoll, Daryl Kraft, Pastor Philip DeCourcy and Kim Gardell have helped make this project a unique resource tool for those seeking to Man Up!

As Scripture reminds us, "Grow in the grace and knowledge of our Lord and Savior Jesus Christ. To Him be the glory both now and forever. Amen" (2 Peter 3:18 NKJV).

FOREWORD

"Where are the men," Dr. Grassi asks. That's a good question and people are asking it more and more. As you read through these pages, you will resonate with what Jim has to say. You'll have many moments of pounding your fist onto the table and saying, "That's right!"

But Grassi doesn't leave us there. He gives us the solution. The solution is Jesus Christ of course, but our Lord commanded us to go further than just knowing Him – He told us to go make disciples. My good friend, Judge Vance Day, says that it takes men to make men. Where are the men? They are all around us – little boys trapped in big, hairy bodies looking for someone to teach them what it means to be truly and beautifully masculine.

In Ayn Rand's novel, Atlas Shrugged, society begins attacking and stealing from the most productive people. When those people begin to remove themselves from society, the intellectuals cheer. Then the nations fall apart, and society begins looking for who will help but no one is left. We see the novel **playing out in** an attack against masculinity today. Men are removing themselves from society through apathy, or obsession with work, sports, pornography…they've lost interest and its beginning to show in alarming ways.

Jesus is the only answer! We need His children to be diligent and relentless in getting the Good News to suffering people. This must start with men discipling other men Because fathers are the key to the family. Fathers who love Jesus have wives who love Jesus and they raise kids who love Jesus. The harvest is great, but the workers are few.

Grassi is calling us all to be workers – the kind of workers to who Jesus greets at the Judgment seat with those awesome words, "Well done!" William F. Buckley said that at times we need someone to stand athwart history and yell, "Stop!" The godless warn that we don't want to be on the wrong side of history. Grassi says, "Yes we do!" The question is, who's with him?

— Ken Harrison,
Chairman of the Board, Promise Keepers

INTRODUCTION

I am only one, but I am one. I cannot do everything, but I can do something. And I will not let what I cannot do interfere with what I can do.
– Edward Everett Hale

Billy is a six-year-old boy whose father was killed two-years earlier during a fierce firefight in Syria while serving with the U.S. Military. Billy's mother is doing her best to raise the young boy and his three-year-old sister, but her husband's absence has left a huge hole in their lives. Among other deep feelings of loss, Billy's mom realizes *it takes a man to show a man how to be a man.*

Billy recently came home from school crying. Billy's teacher is a divorced woman who is very bitter and harbors some "man-issues" in her life. Whether she knows it or not, she seems to relish embarrassing the little boys in her class. She often tells the young boys they are not as smart as the girls and boasts that girls are special while boys are distracting and rambunctious.

The girls out-number the boys in class and they delight in taking their teacher's lead and making fun of the boys. Billy is a quiet, tender-hearted boy who misses the strength his father exuded. With his father gone, Billy's role models are plastic fantasy figures that stand mute on his bedroom dresser.

As Billy's mother tried to comfort him during his melt-down she asked him, "Billy, what happened to you today that was so upsetting?" As Billy wiped the tears away, he whimpered, "Mommy, why do girls hate boys so much?"

Billy is not alone in his feelings. Many grown men feel disrespected, marginalized, and even hated by women. What has happened in our culture that so many men feel lost, lonely and disenfranchised? It appears that men and manhood are under attack.

Consider some of the popular sitcoms from recent years that are leading us into a new way of imaging men: "According to Jim," "Last Man Standing," "Everybody Loves Raymond," "The Office," "All in the Family," and "Home Improvement," just to name a few. All these sitcoms consistently portray men as imbeciles, klutzes, and chauvinistic. Numerous commercials also depict men in a negative light. Another approach has labeled masculinity as "toxic," and seeks to feminize men.

Let me say from the start, I don't believe this antagonism toward men is the result of a "gender war" being propagated by *most women*. Certainly, there are many factors at play here, but I believe we men bear the lion's share of the responsibility. I also think the present distorted view of manhood has its roots in two areas: (1)

the failure of men to pursue godliness, and (2) the vicious attack on men by an angry group of social and politically liberal elements of our society.

Men, we must be willing to first look at our part. For decades, men in general have shirked their responsibilities in the home as husbands and fathers. Do you want to know one reason we men are experiencing this toxicity toward us today?

> *I'll tell you why! Because the Lord witnessed the vows you and your wife made when you were young. But you have not been faithful to her, though she remained your faithful partner, the wife of your marriage vows.*
>
> *Didn't the Lord make you one with your wife? In body and spirit you are His. And what does He want? Godly children from your union. So, guard your heart; remain loyal to the wife of your youth. "For I hate divorce!" says the Lord, the God of Israel. "To divorce your wife is to overwhelm her with cruelty," says the Lord of Heaven's Armies. "So guard your heart; do not be unfaithful to your wife."– Malachi 2:13-16 NLT*

Divorce is rampant, and in its wake, we have left nearly half the households in our nation without a man to protect and provide for his wife and children. While men are not always the ones seeking divorce, the result is the same. Many of the disenchanted and even angry women attacking men today came from a home where a bitter and even toxic mom was left to raise little boys and girls. The children picked up on their mothers' anger over the situation and absorbed much of the venom and pain as their own.

They left the home to strike out into a career with a general anger and disrespect towards men already prominent in their thinking.

Many men lost their way in the pursuit of success by not spending enough time cultivating and discipling their children. Some men gauged their manhood based on success, power, fortune, fame, and an unhealthy leadership style that manipulated and controlled others. That was not a true representation of biblical manhood and it undermined their role as husband and father in the home. I also believe we're experiencing such a backlash against masculinity because of sexual abuse. We're told that one in three girls in the United States are sexually abused before they reach the age of 18, and men are the perpetrators. One in six American women either experience rape or the attempt[1] is made to do so— again by men![2]

And then there's pornography. Oh, I've heard men say, "I'm not hurting anybody by looking at porn. What's the big deal?" The big deal is that a whole human trafficking industry has sprung up to support men's insatiable lust for porn. When a man engages in porn, he is supporting human trafficking of innocent girls and women. He is contributing to their sexual abuse. If that weren't enough, pornography devastates marriages. Can you even imagine what it does to a wife to know that her husband would rather find fulfillment in a virtual prostitute than to love and embrace his own wife? Pornography destroys families, women, girls and the man's soul.

The *second component* of the problem is with a society that is drifting away from a godly culture into a dark hole of narcissistic pleasure and a hostile feminist environment. Society has so distorted what authentic manhood looks like that many men linger in the fog of uncertainty, guilt, shame, despair, loneliness, fear, and anger.

As a culture, our focus is on concerns like global warming, how far we can push discussions on abortion, saving animals, and manipulating politics. Yet, we ignore the development of strong families, which form the foundation of any healthy culture. Meanwhile, homelessness is on the rise. Drug use and suicide continue to soar. In short, we're becoming more and more broken as a society.

We have lost sight of the biblical foundation that this country was founded upon. Instead of our youth embracing and connecting with past generations who gave so much to develop our country, they spend their time idly sending texts to friends who are also clueless about living a successful life. The liberal educators in our schools and colleges teach children to question and explore their sexuality, ignore their parents, and challenge any authority while we medicate them so they can endure their frustrations, intimidation, and boredom.

Our emphasis on technology and social media has changed the way people communicate on a personal level. Face-to-face critical problem-solving and conflict resolution have been replaced with inappropriate and cold texts, tweets, and emails, often leaving the offended party in emotional turmoil. Younger people are more likely to go to Google for answers to complex personal problems than ask their parents for advice.

Many younger men today have confused their dreams and wants with the enabling culture that didn't encourage an appropriate work ethic to achieve their aspirations. The idea of identifying lofty goals and having a plan to attain them is a foreign concept in a society that insists everyone deserves a "participation" trophy.

For the most part, contemporary society and its brokenness can be directly linked to the upstream problem with men. The downstream issues that are negatively impacting our cities and families come from *fatherless* families or households where dad is not emotionally involved in leading his tribe. Consequently, there is a direct link to a myriad of social ills such as homelessness, juvenile delinquency, pornography, poverty, crime, orphans, homosexuality, and a host of emotional disorders.

Friends, we have a moral and spiritual war going on that is as equally devastating as nuclear bombs being dropped on our country. Men must rise-up and become warriors for God and their families or this culture is doomed. We must lovingly project an agenda of hope, strength, courage, and great character to the younger generation.

A boisterous call is going out for godly men who are determined and courageous to go to battle. This is not a physical battle but a spiritual, moral, and cultural one. The apostle Paul heard of their struggles and wrote two letters to the young men involved with the church in Corinth. Paul confronted them with the sin in their culture and the need for corrective action and a clear commitment to Christ. He especially rallied the men to engage with their corrupt culture and the disillusioned leaders who had lost their passion to know God and make Him known.

His admonishment rings true today: *"Be on the alert, stand firm in the faith, act like men, be strong. Let all that you do be done in love."* (1 Corinthians. 16:13-14 ESV) If we are to take back our culture from the wickedness and false doctrines that have permeated the very souls of many men and their families, we should follow the same instructions Paul gave the church of Corinth.

Our battle isn't with the opposite sex, but with our own complacency and disengagement from the political, social, and personal processes that disenfranchise us from creating a worldview that embraces respect, love, hope, and dignity for all. We need to win the battle for the sake of our families, especially our sons, and our country. I believe that God is calling men all over this land to return to Him. Twenty-first century manhood needs to root itself back into the biblical values that create a stable culture. God is calling us to love our wives sacrificially to honor, respect, and protect women in general. God is calling us to father and mentor our children by living under the same roof, to treat them gently, leading them and modeling for them what it means to follow Jesus. Frightened and confused boys like Billy need godly male role models and mentors all around them.

This book presents a discussion of what God intended manhood to look like. It identifies some of the issues, barriers, and generational traits that helped create a chasm between the sexes and age groups. I want to challenge men to evaluate their role in this culture that is presently filled with antagonism, mistrust, and confusion about men and their God-given mission. We will take on some of the myths and misperceptions perpetrated by some politicians, the liberal media, and Hollywood. These entities would have us believe that strong, determined, compassionate, and courageous men are no longer welcome in our "progressive" culture.

This book serves as a catalyst to call men to be men; to behave like real men. Many men are so confused they don't even know how or where to begin. I pray that this book provides some answers and direction. I'm calling on every man reading this book to return to *biblical manhood*. Be the man God created and designed you to be!

Are you with me? Let's demonstrate to our wives and the little girls and women around us what a real man is like—one who protects, provides, and is even willing to lay down his life for them.

Let's Man Up!

Jim

James E. Grassi, D. Min.,
husband, father, grandfather and follower of Jesus

CHAPTER ONE
IN THE BEGINNING

Too many boys and young men have grown up with no positive role models in their immediate family. They have had no one to show them, by modeling a respectful life, how to be a man.

I looked for someone who might rebuild the wall of righteousness that guards the land. I searched for someone to stand in the gap in the wall so I wouldn't have to destroy the land, but I found no one.
– Ezekiel 22:30 NLT

Could it be that God will use people like you and me to help turn the hearts of the children to their fathers and most importantly the hearts of their fathers to their children? — Luke 1:17

WHAT HAPPENED TO AMERICA?

America will never be great again until it addresses the issues impacting the men of this country. Unfortunately, families who are fatherless or have uninvolved fathers are in the majority today. Over 50 million children are being raised by single-parent mothers. Society is suffering because we lack positive male role models. We need men who provide for and protect their families with uncompromising faith, unimpeachable passion, and who strive to become the men God intended them to be. It is the man who is charged with shaping his family and passing on the traditions, heritage, and legacies from previous generations while guiding his family into the future.

If we really want to make America great again, we must put families first and equip them with capable fathers. Men are attacked routinely by the mainstream media, liberal educational institutions, many sitcoms and commercials, and feminist organizations. Despite this, we must better equip, enable, and encourage men to re-establish their role as the leaders of their families.

Unfortunately, too many men have turned in their "parenting cards" and have abandoned their leadership roles as the person who "stands in the gap" for their families. It's as if we have returned to the times that the Old Testament Prophet Ezekiel described.

The Israelites had grown so corrupt that God had sent Babylon's army to destroy Jerusalem and carry its people into captivity in Babylon. Despite all God's warnings through the prophets and His Word, the people had sinned against Him and each other in grievous ways.

In a manner like Ezekiel in his day, we boldly call out the men of our day with the admonishment Ezekiel gave, which came straight from God. "I looked for someone who might rebuild the wall of righteousness that guards the land. I searched for someone to stand in the gap in the wall so I wouldn't have to destroy the land, but I found no one." (Ezekiel 22:30 NLT)

One of the passions driving this project is my desire to engage and equip men with resources and inspiration at whatever place they are in life while also helping them succeed spiritually. For the past four decades, my passion has been to help men grow in Christ. Many other men who faithfully follow Jesus have enriched my life in the process, and now I seek to pass this legacy on to you in this book.

The current events and social phenomena that are leading us away from *biblical manhood* frighten me. Men need encouragement and a pathway to rebuilding their hearts and perspective. It is not normally the custom in Christian writing or preaching to be political. Unfortunately, the politics and social landscape of our current culture have distorted and corrupted many of our religious institutions. Therefore, I find it necessary to take-on the political establishment although some of my colleagues dodge this controversial topic because it might "offend someone" in their congregation or social network. It is weird to me that I often feel Fox News Analyst Tucker Carlson has a better grip on the theology of masculinity than a few of my colleagues wearing a liturgical collar.

During another dark period of American history, a special song became a call to wake up the men of our nation. The inspirational song *Stout-Hearted Men* written by Sigmund Romberg during the Great Depression Era beckoned men to be *stout-hearted, determined, resolute, and committed* to inspire others with truth and hope. Today, it seems like many men have relinquished their spiritual authority and manhood because they lack a Kingdom perspective on how to do life.

Today we have 40-50% of our young male population without a biological father in their home during their formative adolescent years. Instead of *stout-hearted and determined young men,* we see too many weak-kneed, snowflake, pajama boys with an entitlement mentality. These young men need and deserve courageous mentors in their lives who will help guide and direct them to godliness and maturity.

Pastor Tony Evans in his book, *Kingdom Man: Every Man's Destiny, Every Women's Dream,* points out that the world is experiencing devastating effects of having a lower standard of manhood.

> *The deterioration of societies both nearby and around the world has reached an all-time high, while the clarion call for men to come forth to stand for biblical manhood has never rung louder.*

*Our world is on a disparaging path of self-destructive behavior. That must change. Yet that change will not occur unless men will raise standards where God originally placed it.*3

GOD UNIQUELY CREATED US

We read in Genesis that God spoke all the other creations into being, but when it came to man, He shaped, molded, sculpted, and fashioned him in *His Image* (Gen. 1:26-28). God didn't haphazardly form man but created him in His likeness. Our Creator was a thoughtful, loving, creative artist who crafted man in His image.

Unlike all the other things He created, God gave mankind mental and spiritual capacities that enable him to relate to Him and to serve Him. God gave mankind the authority to rule over the rest of creation as His earthly vice-mentors and ambassadors. Man was meant to function like a mirror, reflecting the image of God into creation. God made man and woman different—both physiologically and more importantly, psychologically.

It is interesting to note that the Hebrew word for the creation of man is "formed" from the dust of the earth. He was grounded in a sense to God's foundational platform. Whereas, women were "fashioned" or shaped to be a companion and helpmate to man.

It is God's intent that we really *know* Him. To know Him means that mankind was to please God through intimate relationship. When our perfect relationship with God was broken by disobedience, mankind set out to please Him instead through acts of work, sacrifice, accomplishments, and power. Pastor Eric Mason does an outstanding job analyzing Scripture on this point in his masterful book titled: *Manhood Restored: How the Gospel Makes Men Whole.*

In this work Mason explains:

> *Relationship with God is so central to what it means to be an image bearer that Jeremiah states it is the only thing man can boast about in relation to himself: "Thus, says the Lord of hosts: 'Let not the wise man glory in his wisdom, let not the mighty man glory in his might, nor let the rich man glory in his riches; but let him who glories glory in this, that he understands and knows Me, that I am the Lord, exercising lovingkindness, judgment, and righteousness in the earth. For in these I delight,' says the Lord."*

> *The word know is a term of intimacy. It's the same word used of God's intimate knowledge of the prophet in Jeremiah 1:5. When God restored man through Jesus Christ, the first thing highlighted isn't religion or responsibility, but relationship (John 17:3). The point is that relationship is the most compelling factor driving what it means to be made in the image of God."*[4]

WHAT IS THE PROBLEM?

The truth is that our corrupt model of manhood began in the Garden of Eden. God created man to have relationship with Him, as testified in the book of Genesis:

Then God said, "Let Us make man in Our image, according to Our likeness; let them have dominion over the fish of the sea, over the birds of the air, and over the cattle, over all the earth and over every creeping thing that creeps on the earth."

And the Lord God commanded the man, saying, "Of every tree of the garden you may freely eat; but of the tree of the knowledge of good and evil you shall not eat, for in the day that you eat of it you shall surely die." (Genesis 1:26; 2:16-17 NKJV)

God realized that man needed a companion to share life with, to protect and provide for, to love and cherish, to serve and honor. God then created a beautiful woman. Together they had the perfect relationship with one another and God. But then:

Now the serpent was more cunning than any beast of the field which the Lord God had made. And he said to the woman, "Has God indeed said, 'You shall not eat of every tree of the garden'?"

And the woman said to the serpent, "We may eat the fruit of the trees of the garden; ³ but of the fruit of the tree which is in the midst of the garden, God has said, 'You shall not eat it, nor shall you touch it, lest you die.' " (Genesis 3:1-3 NKJV)

During the dialog with Satan, where was Adam? He was *standing right there and watching*. He didn't defend, he didn't lead, he didn't protect, he didn't communicate truth with his mate. No, he stood and watched. And with no input from her man, Eve became deceived and partook of the forbidden fruit.

God called out to Adam: "Where *are* you?" Adam recognized their disobedience and was ashamed of their nakedness. But instead of admitting *his* failure, he first blamed his wife and then God for his failure! He had failed a second time to protect his wife from harm. He lacked the courage and foresight to stand against Satan, or to humble himself before God and admit his own wrongdoing. It was his prescribed duty to take care of his wife and be her protector.

Since the original sin and throughout history we find that in our most divisive and challenging times too many good men have *not* taken a stand but have stood and watched. They failed to act, protect, provide, and rescue. They failed at being the men God created them to be.

THE FALL OF A NATION

As we read through the Old and New Testaments time and time again, we see the fall of great nations because of moral collapse within their culture. The collapse can be attributed to the failure of the family unit. And in most cases men did not stand up for the values God provided in the Ten Commandments. They were preoccupied with the pursuit of power, fame, and fortune or frightened off by powerful women. Men forgot how to be men and consequently began to disrespect themselves *and* females.

It seems that the demise of our country started on June 25, 1962. The United States Supreme Court decided in Engel v. Vitale to eliminate prayer, arguing that it violated the First Amendment because it represented the establishment of religion. Thus, prayer was taken away from our educational institutions. The eternal measuring rod for morality, civility, and spirituality was replaced with cultural trends, flower children, new-age thinking, feminism, and false gods. Into the gap that was left after the biblical underpinning began to collapse, flowed the unstable philosophy promoted by many liberal educators, movie stars, athletes, and politicians. These warped individuals began to poison the minds of our youth by disrespecting the very Judeo/Christian values that formed the foundation of this country, providing them with the very freedoms they now enjoyed.

Within some of our young people a sense of eternal destiny was lost when our biblically based ethics and morality were thrown under the bus. With the disrespect of our flag and lack of a Pledge of Alliance came a loss of patriotism and national unity. Filling the void left by these foundational pieces of our society came humanism, atheism, and narcissism. Since behavior follows belief children are becoming more undisciplined without godly fathers, educators, and mentors to help direct them towards standards that have everlasting value.

The erosion of values, decency, and common respect created a void that has now been filled with anger, bitterness, disrespect, immorality, and ungodliness. Where were the protectors of truth? What happened to the kind of people who strive to be solid role models (e.g., Roy Rogers, John Wayne, Gene Autrey, Nelson Mandela, Dr. Ben Carson, Billy Graham, Bart Starr, Teddy Roosevelt, Ronald Reagan, Pat Boone, Mr. Rogers)? Isn't it interesting that these men of great character and patriotism are still aired on television with the many re-runs of old programs we love to see because their persona withstood the challenge of time?

Most importantly, too many boys and young men have grown up with no positive role models in their immediate family. They have had no one to show them, by modeling a respectful life, how to be a man; a man who faithfully loves his wife, family, country, and Creator. We have lost many young men because:

- Boys were not raised with their biological fathers
- They hadn't been trained and equipped by a devoted father
- Their father was a poor example for them in their growing up years

Still, other men merely stood by and watched as our country swung away from its biblical foundation. Why? Because we were afraid that we might upset someone or make them angry, or we didn't have the time and tools to stand our ground. Too many men have either abdicated their leadership roles in the family or have been pushed out by disenchanted women who are angry with their situation.

It is also true that many men are sleepwalking into the future. They lack purpose, haven't made the effort to plan their lives or strive for noble goals.

As Dr. Crawford Loritts, Jr., Senior Pastor of the Fellowship Bible Church in Roswell, Georgia stated:

Manhood has fallen on hard times. So many men have been beaten-up by the past, mired in the consequences of bad choices, and confused and disoriented by a culture committed to redefining manhood so that we can cover the fractures and disguise the torment.[5]

If you believe I'm a disenchanted male chauvinist, you are wrong! I was at the forefront of supporting women within the institutions I was associated with in the 1970's and 1980's. I encouraged women to become involved in leadership roles within these organizations. I firmly believe in the equality of opportunity and pay for women. I have no problem with godly men or women in politics and leading major corporations. And I even married the woman who beat me in a high school election for president of the student body.

THE WORLD IN WHICH WE LIVE

Before we can unpack the subject of manhood, we must explore the current environment that is so challenging for many males. I make no apologies for this necessary side trip. We can't evaluate men and manhood in a vacuum, but we must look at it through the eyes of current demographics reflecting our culture. My thoughts in this work have evolved from the study of scores of articles, dozens of books, sermons, and volumes of statistical data that all point to a systemic *war on men in America.*

In March 2009 President Obama created a White House Council on Women and Girls. Colleges have core programs on Women's Studies or Issues. Where is the focus upon men and fatherhood? Billy Graham once stated, "A good father is one of the most unsung, unpraised, unrewarded, unnoticed, and yet one of the most valuable assets in our society."

We often see the "minority card" or "victim card" played when it comes to most discussions surrounding the impact women are having on the country. We owe a debt of gratitude to Dr. Richard T. Hise, Professor of Marketing at Texas A&M University and author of several books. His exhaustive work titled *The War Against Men – Why Women are Winning* dispels many of the myths that the Radical Feminist Movement is hiding behind. The following is a summary of some of his more revealing points:

- More women than men are in the civilian workforce
- Women are entering and graduating from college at a higher rate than men
- Females are outperforming and receiving more management positions than men
- Women are reversing the sexual codes of dress – they want to look and act like men
- Disproving the myth women aren't in leadership positions, more women are in governmental and military positions of power than ever before

- As a symbol of power more women are smoking cigars than their counterparts

- In Protestant churches up to 80% of the attendees are frequently women and many are the pastor or head major committees of the church

- Women control more wealth in the country than ever before

- Women dominate the media and literary fields; thereby controlling much of the negative anti-male information the nation is consuming

More females want to act like males because of their own dissatisfaction with themselves and their role in life. Radical feminists have demeaned their own gender by making women who submit to their husbands and/or are "stay at home" moms feel inferior.[6]

Research clearly demonstrates that women are enjoying more power and influence across several important fronts. Most of this power has come as the influence of males has declined.

THE FEMINIST MOVEMENT

The early feminist movement got hijacked. Many good things (for both men and women) came out of the original arguments known as the feminist movement. Women had been misrepresented, underpaid, overworked, abused, and too often treated as second-class citizens in the workplace. The movement made some good strides. Then, sadly, the movement got hijacked by leftists who burned their bras and convinced the world that men are not only pigs, but they are not necessary anymore. Men were not even *needed* in the eyes of these women leaders of the movement. So, instead of women just telling men they were pigs, women essentially became the very essence of the qualities or characteristics they opposed in men.

One example of the blame game came in a recent broadcast. Lately, we have heard a great deal about global warming. On April 4, 2019 a Fox News Program aired a commentary by Mark Steyn in which he discussed a "new" research paper[7] that blames "toxic masculinity" for global warming. In his analysis of the report Tucker Carlson stated, "Due to 'toxic masculinity,' apparently too many men like driving big gas-guzzling trucks, they won't use reusable grocery bags, and they like to build campfires in the outdoors. All of those are activities that impact our environment and have contributed to global warning. Therefore, men again are to blame.

American economist, author, and conspiracy theorist Paul Craig Roberts once said, "It is even more the case now that radical feminists have succeeded in making some women feel that they have a moral obligation to hate men with the same intensity that Nazis felt for Jews and Communists for the bourgeoisie."[8]

POLITICAL CORRECTNESS

This book wasn't meant to be politically correct (P.C.) but biblically correct (B.C.). I believe we have lost our way when it comes to understanding manhood. Today, many of the news media, televisions sitcoms and commercials, and politicians have depicted men as stupid, uninformed, disconnected, and nothing but a sperm bank for aggressive, angry women to perpetuate their agendas.

Many of these sources tell us that if you happen to be born with the XY male chromosome you are presumed guilty, ignorant, and hopeless. I'm sick and tired of the war on masculinity! To some in this country, maleness and manhood have become synonymous with radial conservatism, bullying, male chauvinism and sexual harassment. The average guy I speak with tells me that if he doesn't want to be discriminated against, he must accept a Progressive Agenda filled with anti-masculine, male-toxic characterizations, and slanderous attitudes against manly men.

The radical feminists say their worldview is the only one that matters. This is not only selfish and narcissistic but confuses future generations about God-given roles of His creation. And it lacks forgiveness, grace, and understanding. The bitterness of Progressives now tells us that their subjective experience should determine the standards of conduct and even the way we greet people. They have set the agenda for all of us to follow. The problem is the agenda and definitions for appropriateness change almost daily.

Even organizations like the Boy Scouts believe that to obtain the necessary funding and to be P.C. they needed to become integrated. One of the last bastions where "boys could be boys" and a place where young men could gather some skills about the responsibilities of manhood is now crippled by political correctness.

Now girls can join Boy Scouts to further complicate the lives of confused, sexually frustrated young boys trying to develop outdoor coping skills that build good self-confidence and leadership skills. How come boys aren't allowed into Camp Fire Girls or the Girl Scout program?

Some of the younger guys I've encountered feel a little traumatized and demasculinized in relationships with a strong young woman in authority over them. They are intimidated and feel discriminated against if they share any "manly attitudes" about their passions and interests in hunting, fishing, shooting sports, cars, trucks, the outdoors, etc. That is very unfortunate, because being in relationship with a strong woman can be a very positive thing if women acknowledge and respect the way a man processes things.

Think about this... we have evolved into such a *politically correct* society that we might offend someone's sensibilities by clapping or audibly showing our pleasure with something. Progressives tell us we now should do a "jazz wave" instead. We also shouldn't use capital letters in our emails because it means we are angry or shouting at people—especially if a man is sending an email to a woman. If that wasn't crazy enough, we shouldn't crowd a person's personal space by hugging them. We should treat everyone like they have a cold. C'MON PEOPLE - GET A GRIP!

What is a little energetic grammar-school-aged boy supposed to do with all his energy? According to today's many educators, boys are supposed to act like a little girl and be quiet and don't show any loud emotion.

WHY "RADICAL PROGRESSIVE WOMEN" CAN OVERWHELM MANY MEN

It seems that to be a Progressive Woman means you must be hostile to men. That is an agenda item we see clearly played out before us every day in the news media. It became particularly apparent during the 2016 Political Campaigns and during the 2018 Justice Kavanaugh hearings for Supreme Court.

The Radical Feminist Movement, in part, set off the Progressive Movement as a way for one party to obtain votes over another. The Radical Feminist Movement was more than forbidding men to open the door for women. It set into motion a series of actions and events that reshaped the political and social landscape and created an atmosphere of outright anger and distrust towards all men. That, in combination with too many men who were absorbed with trying to be successful at the cost of being the dynamic leader and protector in their family, has led to a generation of ill-equipped young men who have little passion to look beyond social media and Xbox games for relationships.

The *Me-Too Movement* has also projected itself into all levels of culture that now presumes that all men are evil and at fault for a host of social ills impacting our country; therefore, they are no longer equipped or capable of being effective leaders. This is a myth that creates additional mistrust of men in general. People need to realize that when women file multiple false accusations against good men who are not guilty then it drowns out the legitimate cases that deserve the full attention and legal review of the judicial system. Also, those women should be held liable for their false accusations and prosecuted.

Men have either relinquished their roles as leaders or let the Progressive Agenda take away from them the hallmarks of manhood that once provided the stable platform for launching young men into the world. Some would even go as far to say we are no longer equipped with the skill set to be effective husbands, fathers, employees, and godly role models. They contend that men are unable to respectfully lead their families and communities to effective change.

Instead, we have many young men who have been encouraged to be softer, mellower, and more feminine in their lives and behavior. We now have a society that suggests that one's maleness or masculinity is *toxic*. Gillette Razor Company is trying to promote their products by apologizing for their past commercials depicting strong men. They are now suggesting that there is something toxic about masculinity. Really?

Peggy Noonan, former speech writer for Ronald Reagan, had this to say in her 2003 book, *A Heart, A Cross and A Flag*: "It is hard to be a man. I am certain of it; to be a man in this world is not easy. I know what you are thinking, but it's not easy to be a woman either, and you are right. But women get to complain and make others feel bad about their plight. Men have to suck it up and remain good natured, constructive, and helpful...." [9]

I want to help restore a cultural climate in this country that enhances the importance, dignity, and value of biblical manhood. In order to do this, we need to *Man Up and Act Like Men by Being Strong* on many issues impacting our culture. We must remember that investing in our younger men with solid biblical teaching on manhood is a good thing. *After all, it is easier to build a strong young man than it is to repair the broken adult.*

DISCUSSION QUESTIONS:

1. What is the image God had in mind when He created mankind (Genesis 1 & 2)?

2. What individuals come to mind when thinking
   about a man who is balanced, courageous, bright,
   a lover of his family, kind-hearted, has a strong
   temperament, and is a leader of others (Moses, King
   David, Solomon, Apostle Paul, Jesus)?

3. How do you view women and men in
   today's culture?

4. What can you do to become more involved
   with creating a culture that respects both women
   and men?

CHAPTER TWO
BE ALERT, BE STRONG!

Act as men; do what your nature summons you to do. It sets before us as the standard and measure of our duty not merely what is peculiar to ourselves individually, nor merely what has been in fact exemplified by others, but the totality of human nature—man as he was made by his Creator, and as he was fitted and designed to be.
– Professor William Henry Green

Be watchful, stand firm in the faith, act like men, be strong. Let all that you do be done in love.
– 1 Corinthians 16:13-14 ESV

You are to conduct yourself as a man in the way God defines manhood, not the way the world defines it. This truth needs to be heard in our day when men are so ridiculed and vilified. God needs godly, strong, courageous men. – James MacDonald

In the late 1990s and early 2000s I had the privilege of serving in the capacity of character coach/chaplain with the Oakland Raiders. Because of my passion to encourage men in their faith and character I had a few opportunities to visit with other professional teams as well. From my association with NFL football, I eventually ended up writing three books on football and faith based upon my study, experience, and observations of the game and team members.

There are many wonderful players I could use for an illustration in this chapter, but one guy stands out among all the greats I've known. Steve Wisniewski #76, nicknamed "The Wiz," played at his position as left guard 13 seasons with the Oakland Raiders and was an eight-time All-Pro in his career. Frankly, he should be in the Hall of Fame, but because he is so humble and not a self-promoter, his chances are not good.

He faithfully protected quarterbacks like Jay Schroeder, Jeff Hostetler, Jeff George, and Rich Gannon. Wiz is a model citizen, a consummate professional, and a very tough load for any opposing team to handle. *Sports Illustrated* recognized him as one of the toughest guys in football because of his great strength and perseverance. Among his Oakland Raider teammates, Steve is known for his competitive spirit and dynamic power.

Despite his toughness he would always survey the field after a play to see what teammate needed some help back to their feet or an encouraging word. If one of his teammates was being bullied or got into a fight, Steve would go to defend and protect his friends.

Steve had a tenacious spirit. He wasn't going to quit until the whistle blew. It didn't matter if the play wasn't coming his way. If a defensive player was in his zone that guy was going to end up on the ground or nursing a deep bruise the following week.

When I think about his dedication and commitment to excellence, I also recall the time he ran a marathon. His 6'4", 290-pound frame is not exactly suited for distance running, but on May 18, 1997 he ran and finished the Olympia, Washington, Marathon. Very few men his size have ever finished a 26.2-mile run in five hours and thirty-three minutes.

As I became good friends with Steve and his family, I continued to study what separated him from other offensive linemen. Why did the quarterbacks and owners consider him such an asset? Clearly, his peers recognized Steve's toughness, intelligence, dependability, and durability, but beyond those traits what were the intangibles?

THE REAL MEASURE OF A MAN

Some of Steve's traits that stood out to me are found in the verse at the beginning of this chapter that Paul wrote nearly two-thousand years ago. Steve was always alert, watchful, and on-guard the minute the ball was snapped. His head was like a pivot–rotating 180 degrees every second. He could see the blitzing defensive back or linebacker before they even crossed the line of scrimmage. His attentiveness to possible danger and subsequent block saved many quarterbacks from jarring tackles.

Another quality was his ability to stand firm in the pocket, refusing to give ground to the advancing linemen. He played against some of the greats like Cortez Kennedy, Reggie White, Richard Seymore, and Warren Sapp but Steve battled fiercely in defending his position.

Beyond his extraordinary play on the field, his mature and uncompromising faith in the Lord was the thing I most remember. He was unashamed to be a strong man of faith and willing to discuss his passion for God's Word with anyone who would listen. He never apologized for being a committed follower of Christ.

He loved his family and teammates with a sacrificial heart. He looked for every opportunity to serve others. I never was embarrassed about Wiz's behavior. Off the field he was a gentle giant and respected others. He was a man you would be proud and honored to know.

Steve clearly stood out among his team members and the whole football culture. But not all football players, or for that matter men, strive to portray Steve's spiritual example. Unfortunately, we find corruption, greed, self-centeredness, immorality, and a host of other vices within all walks of life. In fact, some of the recent scandals and moral failures of prominent professional football players reminds me of the new Christians struggling in the ancient city of Corinth.

A PLACE CALLED CORINTH

After Christ's death and resurrection, Paul and his co-workers established a Christian church in Corinth. The city was a major cosmopolitan area, a seaport and major trade center located in the region of Achaia (modern Greece). The combination of the difficult geography and the culture filled with idolatry and im-morality created a unique environment for the early Christians to spread the Word of God. The apostle Paul also found it chal-lenging to establish a church among the many Gentiles who lived in Corinth.

In his frustration, Paul stated, "I appeal to you, dear brothers and sisters, by the authority of our Lord Jesus Christ, to live in harmony with each other. Let there be no divisions in the church. Rather, be of one mind, united in thought and purpose." (1 Corinthians. 1:10 NLT)

Much like America today, the Christians in Corinth were strug-gling with their culture. Surrounded by corruption, political unrest, and every conceivable sin, they felt the pressure to adapt and accept the immoral trends impacting society. While they knew of the freedom in Christ, it was difficult for them to understand Christ's teaching on sexuality, idolatry, marriage, women in the church, and the gifts of the Spirit.

Consequently, Paul confronted them about their sin and immature faith. He challenged them to get a spiritual grip on their Christian faith and to stand firm in their convictions as many were falling back into their old behaviors and cultural distractions.

A WARNING MESSAGE

Paul summarized his first letter to the new church in Corinth with a powerful verse that we based this work upon: "Be watchful, stand firm in the faith, act like men, be strong. Let all that you do be done in love." (1 Corinthians. 16:13-14 ESV)

His exhortation had five key points. And much like "The Wiz" we need to be ever diligent and faithful. In order to keep with the central theme of this book, let's explore this verse at a deeper level. We will see that this admonition from Paul shows us how we should Man Up!

Depending upon the Bible translation or commentary you use, we find that to Be Watchful means that we need to be ever on guard, diligent, mindful, and alert. Its basic meaning is to be awake, used in the sense of "watch out." Paul is challenging the passive men in the early Corinthian church to be alert and watchful against the divisive spirit, heresy, corruption, and pride that was prevalent in their community!

If we are to carry out God's will in our lives, then we must acknowledge the evil forces of today's world. This means we can't be distracted from being fully attentive to what might cause harm or calamity to our families, churches, and ourselves.

Real men can only change what they see. Back to our football illustration: No matter how great a quarterback or offensive lineman, there is always a blind spot, something in your area that you can't see. That's when the quarterback usually takes a devastating hit.

So, it is with a real man of God. We think we have all the defensive linemen accounted for in a blocking scheme then a blitzing linebacker messes up everything. As men march forward in life, we are aware of the temptations around us, we believe our conduct is in order. Then, out of nowhere we are blindsided with an attack from Satan. As an example: A new gal is hired to work next to your office, and she refuses to dress respectfully. What do we do? We need to always stay alert that attacks can come in a variety of ways.

A Christian is always in danger, and therefore should always be watchful; but the danger is greater at times and under some circumstances. The Corinthians were in great danger in many ways: they bickered and fought with each other; they were inconsistent in following Jesus; and they tolerated false teachers among them. These deceivers tried to corrupt their faith at its very roots, thus destroying virtue and piety. Surely in such dangerous circumstances they desperately needed to be watchful and alert.[10]

Stand firm in the faith. The original meaning of this concept was a military phrase for holding one's position. In the illustration of "The Wiz," we described how he fought to stand firm and steadfast taking on the opposing defense. In fact, he developed a unique balancing program with a special half round balance platform before others thought of that idea. He developed his feet and legs to stand firmly in the battle.

As men of God we must develop the agility and balance to our lives that centers us on God's plan for our lives. We need to develop the skills to be faithful in standing firm and strong on social and faith issues impacting our lives and families.

"In the faith" refers to Christian truth or Christian doctrine. If a Christian wants to remain secure in his faith, he must be on guard for false teachings and Satanic attacks. And the greater the danger, the greater the vigilance is needful for the security to live a pure life. Paul urges the young Christians to *stand fast in the faith*, to keep their ground, to adhere to the revelation of God, and not exchange it for the wisdom of the world. Nor should we allow ourselves to be corrupted by the world but stand for the faith of the Gospel and maintain it even unto death. We are to stand in the faith, to live in the profession of it and not yield to anything that would alter it.[11]

It also suggests that we remain steadfast in our trust (faith) in Christ. Our personal relationship with God requires prayer, meditation,

Bible study, personal reflection, and accountability. We need other believers in our life to mentor and guide us along life's journey.

A follower of Christ should be fixed in the faith of the gospel, and never desert nor renounce it. It is by this faith alone that he will be able to keep his ground in an hour of temptation. It is by faith that we stand (2 Co. 1:24). It is by this faith that we must overcome the world (1 John. 5:4), both when it flatters and when it frowns, when it tempts and when it terrifies. We must stand therefore in the faith of the gospel, if we would maintain our integrity.[12]

Act like men was an expression Paul used in this verse. He was not trying to be chauvinistic, but to simply express that God designed men to be the protectors and providers for their families. While there are many very capable and strong women, Paul suggests a contrast to being childish or immature in one's mindset. The Greek language implies that *both maturity and courage* are important to spiritual responsibility and manhood.

Paul advises them to act like men, and be strong:

> *Act the manly, firm, and resolved part: behave strenuously, in opposition to the bad men who would divide and corrupt you, those who would split you into factions or seduce you from the faith: be not terrified nor inveigled by them; but show yourselves men in Christ, by your steadiness, by your sound judgment and firm resolution.*[13]

Fourthly, Paul encourages Christian men to **be strong**. Traditionally, a man is expected to be strong, such as taking responsibility for one's actions, displaying bravery or toughness in the face of adversity, providing for one's family, etc. Being strong often suggests too that we *brave it up – become daring.*

When the opposition throws *the blitz* at us, we need to stiffen our resolve by being strong. I'm convinced that trials and tribulations in life help build our character and strength while allowing us to assist others who might have the same challenges. A myth that has penetrated the hearts and minds of many people is that life isn't supposed to be tough. We look at hardships and challenges as though they were unexpected anomalies in pursuing success. That isn't even biblical let alone reality. Read the biographies and biblical accounts of the trials and struggles many great men faced. See how it shaped their character and commitment. Hebrews 11 is a good place to start.

Anyone who has been through hardships realizes that we learn lessons and gain experience that help shape our character and stiffen our spine. As James the half-brother of Jesus testified, "My brethren, count it all joy when you fall into various trials, knowing that the testing of your faith produces patience." (James 1:2-3 NKJV)

Be strong in taking on challenges to your faith, integrity, and heritage. Don't let the trends in our culture and political correctness ambush you into thinking you are misinformed or in the minority. Use your strength of character and resolve to model a Christ-like life to those spectators who have given up.

One of my favorite non-biblical quotes comes from President Teddy Roosevelt, "Far better is it to dare mighty things, to win glorious triumphs even though checkered by failure than to rank with those poor spirits who neither enjoy nor suffer much because they live in the gray twilight that knows neither victory nor defeat."

Let all that you do be done in love. In a religious and cultural situation as dynamic, diverse, and problematic as Corinth, Paul's teaching about love is crucial. Their divisions and strife, selfishness and greed needed to be throttled back by a love that looks at the well-being of the brotherhood. Without love and grace, we cannot effectively model God's will or way. Earlier in his letter to the church in Corinth, Paul reminds us in the love chapter, "And now abide faith, hope, love, these three; but the greatest of these *is* love." (1 Corinthians. 13:13 NKJV)

Paul wanted the Corinthians to remember the importance of a theme that he had emphasized many times in this epistle - *love*. He wanted them always to show love in **everything**. This reminder was very important for a church riddled with strife. Paul had exalted love as the highest ideal in this epistle. He reiterated this ideal so the Corinthians would not forget it. Love for God and their neighbors was to motivate and govern everything they did.

THE SEX TALK

When we think about love in the context of our maleness are minds are naturally drawn to sex. The Sex Talk we may have been given or have provided to our children is a little different today because of the changing cultural patterns that are consuming our nation.

It is appropriate to talk about this subject in the discussion of biblical manhood because it is examined in Scripture. We are commanded by God to procreate, "be fruitful and multiply–bring forth abundantly and fill the earth." (Gen. 1:28 NKJV)

Apparently, to some, it doesn't matter how God created us in the womb. They believe you have the right to change or reframe your sexual orientation and have all the entitlements, including who and how they can bear children. And should you publicly object to these cultural trends in the workplace or in a medical situation you can now be sued for discrimination.

Businesses must comply by creating transgender policies and restrooms to accommodate those who desire to reframe their sexual orientation. As men we are supposed to sit idly by while our wives, daughters, or granddaughters are in a rest room when a male enters claiming he is really a *she* at that moment in time.

Women who fought so hard to get the Title 9 Act in place so that women could receive the attention and funding for their sporting activities are now watching males, who converted to females, win over biological women on the field of play.

Today, we are being told by the Progressive Movement that males should now be allowed and even encouraged to become the mothers to their young. Doctors are looking into ways that a man can carry a child to term, and have it delivered by "C-section."

This is for those poor lost males who think that motherhood should be enjoyed by any male desiring to be a woman.

Research by people such as Dr. Michael Gurian, *Saving our Sons*, Dr. Leonard Sax, *Boys Adrift and Girls on Edge*, and Jed Diamond, *12 Rules for Good Men*, proves that God's design for men and women is different even from the development and construction of our brains. When institutions don't allow boys to be boys and girls to be girls because of how our Creator wired our brains then they are trying to alter God's plan for humanity.

Friends, we are fearfully and wonderfully made by our Creator (Psalm. 139:14) so that there would be clear distinctions between the sexes. No man can handle or replace the compassion, wisdom, commitment, and hard work it takes to be a stay-at-home mother.

In his extensive research and subsequent article Dr. Hagie Levine of The Hebrew University in Jerusalem recently demonstrated that "Male Sperm and Testosterone Count Has Fallen By 50% in 40 Years" due to several sociological and behavioral trends that have change how males function.

The chemicals absorbed from our foods and the lifestyle of the typical western male is marked by significant changes over their parents and grandparent's generations. Males today are more sedentary, absorbing more drugs and smoking products, consuming more alcoholic beverages, involved in pornography, and becoming more obese. All these can be linked in part to male depression about how they are perceived in a dominant female culture. These factors are directly connected to the ability of males to procreate as effectively as males from previous generations.

We need to change the way we handle these attacks on our gender. We must reclaim the biblical roles and character of maleness. God wants us to take a stand against those who would try to alter His plan for men and women.

FIVE POWERFUL COMMANDS

Prof. William Henry Green in his essay Christian Manliness says:

Evoke your dormant energies; put forth the powers that are within you; stifle not the noble emotions that stir your breast; act up to your real capacity; fulfill your own high conceptions and aspirations; achieve results worthy of yourself, such as you can review with satisfaction and expose to others without shame… Act as men; do what your nature summons you to do. It sets before us as the standard and measure of our duty not merely what is peculiar to ourselves individually, nor merely what has been in fact exemplified by others, but the totality of human nature—man as he was made by his Creator, and as he was fitted and designed to be.[14]

As he closes his first letter to the young church in Corinth, the apostle Paul gives us five final commands: be alert, stand firm, act like a mature man, strong, and loving. Let's remember these five traits as we Man Up! for Jesus.

In his workbook *Act Like Men* by James MacDonald he sums up godly manhood with this statement:

> *At the heart of these commands (1 Corinthians. 16:13-14) is the phrase we're focusing on: Act Like Men. Or, as some might say, "man up!" The phrase doesn't mean we should act in the Hollywood sense of the word. God doesn't want actors. God doesn't want posers or impostors. In this passage, the word act means to conduct yourself. You are to conduct yourself as a man in the way God defines manhood, not the way the world defines it. This truth needs to be heard in our day when men are so ridiculed and vilified. God needs godly, strong, courageous men.[15]*

Maybe we can take on the characteristics of "The Wiz" and become an All-Pro man of God in every aspect of our life. It requires discipline, determination, perseverance, courage, focus, and great faith.

DISCUSSION QUESTIONS:

1. When God wants something done, He usually
   gets a man to do it. What can we learn by studying
   Ezekiel 22?

2. Why is it important for us to be *watchmen* for our
   families and communities? Read Ezekiel 33:1-6.

3. What does real *strength of character* look like? What
   does God's Word say about it? Ephesians 6:10; 2
   Timothy 2:1; Mark 12:29-31; 2 Corinthians 12:9.

CHAPTER THREE
WHERE ARE THE MEN?

As goes the husband or father, so goes the family.
As goes the family, so goes the nation.

Similarly, encourage the young men to be self-controlled. In everything set them an example by doing what is good. In your teaching show integrity, seriousness and soundness of speech that cannot be condemned, so that those who oppose you may be ashamed because they have nothing bad to say about us.
– Titus 2:1-8

As never before, we need capable, strong men of God to disciple their kids and become the spiritual leaders within their families, churches, and communities.

In 1910 the World Mission Conference was held in Edinburgh, Scotland. The conference marked a turning point in ecumenical missionary movement because it represented just about the last moment when 'worldwide biblical Christianity' could in any meaningful sense be equated with the brand of Christianity seen in Europe and North America.

Major Protestant, Anglican denominations, and missionary societies, predominantly from North America and Northern Europe, sent 1,215 representatives to *Edinburgh*, Scotland. No *Eastern Orthodox* or *Roman Catholic missionary* organizations were invited.[16]

The formal title of this conference should be called the "third ecumenical missionary conference," because the first and the second had already taken place in London in 1888 and New York in 1900 respectively.[17]

With very poor leadership and a step away from biblical truths, the conference was deemed a spiritual disaster. Quickly, the disappointment spread around the world and most evangelicals realized that their hopes for an ecumenical revival were extinguished.

A lone Scottish woman and missionary pioneer named Mary Slesser (The White Queen of Calabar) was in Calabar, Africa when she heard the disappointing news of the conference. As an abused child of an alcoholic father she had hoped that the male leadership of the conference would stand strong on the biblical principles that led her into ministry. She was an itinerant evangelist and fought against the local customs of witchcraft and liberal teachings. Known as a courageous defender of the Gospel and hearing about the liberalization of the conference churches she asked the question that still rings true today, "Where are the men?"[18]

Where are the men? Men who would courageously stand for the teachings found in the Gospel. Men who would stay connected to family and not vacate their responsibilities as the leaders, protectors, and providers of their families. Men who would push back against immoral and corrupt teachings that erode the culture. Men who are passionate about their calling and seek to be the leaders in their homes, communities, and churches. Men who would stop playing at being perpetual adolescents.

Today, many are asking the same question. In a nation that is quickly becoming a feminist society—where are the men? Too many young people don't want to grow up. We are seeing boys in men's bodies.

To cap it off, recently in an interview with *Axios*, which aired on HBO, California Governor Gavin Newsome was asked about a past statement he made regarding toxic masculinity, where he said, "The most dangerous words in the English language are 'man up,' 'be a man,' and 'don't be a sissy.'" He alleges that those words are toxic and might offend transgenders and effeminate men. According to him manning up is harsh and cruel to sensitive men, as though only the effeminate are sensitive.[19]

I wonder if the governor thought about the kind of tough and daring men it took to build the Golden Gate and Bay Bridges? Or the brave sailors and airman who defended the Bay Area in the various military bases in that region during World War II? Or the kind of guys it took to build all the irrigation canals and dams that provide water to millions? Think about all the craftsmen who chiseled on marble and granite artwork that adorns this great state. These men weren't Peter Pan—Pajama Boys! They weren't sissies. They were all men and proud to be contributing to society by risking their lives for the betterment of society. These stout-hearted men weren't living in Never-Never Land like the Governor of California.

A CHANGING CULTURE

Today, we are experiencing an increase in a variety of crimes and inappropriate behaviors. The demise of our contemporary culture can be directly linked to the brokenness of men today. The plight of the inner cities, unemployment, crime, poverty, abuse of women, angry youth acting out, and a host of other social problems are the result of unfaithful men, broken families, fatherless homes, and ill-equipped fathers providing terrible role models for their children. The failure of young people to launch into life as responsible adults comes as a direct result of the absence of positive male leadership in the home.

Unless our culture begins to refocus its agenda on godly values and rebuilding the home, we can expect there to be no restoration of our nation. There is a cancer of the soul and spirit that is eating away at the dreams, hopes, aspirations, and families that make up the fabric of our society. When men fail everyone fails.

We need to invest in building committed, dedicated men who are inspired and led by God's Word to engage the hostile philosophies and immorality that has crept into every facet and institution of American life. Committed men follow Jesus and fulfill their purpose and destiny in their generation (Acts 13:36).

Civility, bravery, courage, nobility, and kindness are typically foreign to most young men today. They associate these character traits with a lost generation of stuffy old folks. The horrifying increase of mass shootings are indicative of a culture that has lost its way. In almost every case, the shooter was a male who had a "father wound," because they weren't loved, nurtured, and guided by a committed dad.

We cannot blame any one person or political party for the misery of what we see and hear in our local newspapers and on the news. The core of our problems stem from the mass exodus of men leaving their families and offspring to fend for themselves.

Our moral compass has been broken ever since 1963 when the Bible was taken out of the schools. This paved the way for a more liberal society that no longer valued God's teachings about faith, family, and building a strong household. The deepest longings a person can have is to know God and develop an intimate relationship with Him. When educational and political leaders tell us that this is no longer a value or important, mankind begins trying to fill that void with the pursuit of materialism, lusts, fantasy, idolatry, and entertainment.

Forty years ago, only two percent of the population said they had no faith. Today, over 25% of our nation is feeling hopeless and without faith in a God.

Tucker Carlson in his book *Ship of Fools* projects some demographics about our culture that help us understand how so many men and boys are drifting into mediocrity and avoiding becoming self-sufficient, independent adults that can make positive contributions to society.

- Men are being taught in most schools and through the liberal media to deny their own biology. There is a great deal of confusion among younger men as to their masculinity and what it means to be a biblical man of God.
- Seven million American men from 25-54 no longer have jobs. This represents ten percent of the potential male workforce.
- The average male between 30-54 years of age takes ten medications a day to cope with their mental and physiological issues associated with their perceived failure as a man.
- Ninety percent of the inmates incarcerated are men.

- More women graduate from college and get doctorate degrees in their chosen field than men.

- Many boys trying to be men are being taught by single-parent mothers and their biological sisters.

- Seventy-five percent of young boys are considered obese or overweight from lack of activity and the pursuit of video games. They have become couch potatoes.

- Women outnumber men on the mission field two-to-one and have become leaders in many denominations.

- Too many men are playing at being a man instead of being a man. Thirty-four-year-old males are the biggest consumers of video games and watch cartoons more than news programs.

- Seventy-five percent of suicides in America are males who believe there is no hope.

- Women now constitute most professional workers in the United States.

- Too many men feel unhappy, unhealthy, unfulfilled, unreliable, unholy, and are governed by self-interest.[20]

Kevin DeYoung stated:

We have expected nothing out of the young generation so that's what we get. A couple of generations ago, twenty-year-old men were getting married, starting families, working at real jobs, fighting the Nazi's. Today, thirty-five-year-olds are hanging around on Facebook, trying to find direction. We have coddled them instead of challenging them.

Men are not making the transition from boyhood to manhood. Too many young guys are still at home wasting away their lives on social media, video games, and taking advantage of the generosity of their parents. Those who are stuck or wedged between adolescence and manhood are not embracing manhood as a journey. There are many things we *can* do in life but there are some things we *must* do in life so we can be what we need to be in life. Young men need to focus upon being mastered by the Master. Men can be given to irresponsibility, but ultimately that approach to life becomes a vortex of hopelessness and despair.

WHAT IS AT STAKE?

It has been said, "As goes the family, so goes the nation." Our government has invested billions of dollars to help shape the educational system and social networks. Our progressive media believes that it is more important to be "politically correct" than to uphold the values of decency and truth. Our social, economic, and political systems lack reverence and respect for the biblically based ideals our founding fathers identified in our governing documents.

Can you believe that 41% or more of children will be going to bed this evening in a home with no biological father? When you contemplate this disturbing statistic, it is no mystery why so many kids are having difficulty in school, are prone to juvenile delinquency, teen pregnancy, sexual identity issues, etc.

As never before, we need capable, strong men of God to disciple their kids and become the spiritual leaders within their families, churches, and communities. One could say, "As goes the husband or father, so goes the family, church, or government." Again, it starts with relationship. Mentoring, discipling, and modeling are terms that cannot be replaced with governmental mandates or a social gospel.

THE FAILURE OF THE CHURCH

On any given Sunday in most churches across America, the audience will have fewer than 39-percent males.[21] In Europe, male participation rates are much worse, around five percent.[22] The most disturbing news suggests that as many as ninety percent of the boys who are being raised in the church will abandon it on or before their eighteenth birthday. Many of these boys will never return to the faith.[23]

We have many articulate communicators whose Sunday messages inspire people to feel good about themselves, but few are the pastors who preach powerful messages that move people to action to fully commit themselves to the principles of discipleship. There are some Twenty-First Century pastors, teachers, and leaders who consistently talk about and model biblical truths about the primary focus of our faith—discipleship—but their voices are being drowned out amidst the idle chatter of liberal theology and "feel good" religion. Many of our younger preachers care more about entertaining people with loud music, smoke-filled stages, skinny jeans, and cleverly worded sound bites that, from a theological perspective, are an inch deep and a mile wide.

We need to re-visit what it means to be a "true disciple." We need a fresh look at what Christ taught about discipleship. In today's vernacular First Century discipleship would best be described as Spiritual Mentoring. We need to rescue our faith, re-purpose our men, and re-discover how Spiritual Mentors can play a critical role in bringing the church back to its original purpose.

My research shows that one of the greatest needs a retired man has is to still be relevant and to pass along his life experiences to others. One of the greatest needs most young men have is to have a mentor in their lives. Discipleship is a relational process that requires people to become actively involved in their faith. It is the men who will lead their families back to faith. It is men who can help save the Christian Church from the challenges that other religions are placing on our culture. Devoted and active men are the ones who can passionately change the direction of our culture and its destructive patterns that are leading us into chaos and de-spair. And, most importantly, men are commanded by God to be the leaders in the home, church, and community.

Young men need to get on track and seek out being mentored by a responsible man. They need to embrace manhood as a journey and process. The church needs to encourage them by providing opportunities for intergenerational ministry to happen. It must be intentional and dynamic while providing an encouraging and safe environment for men to relate to other men. Life is a team sport. We need each other for encouragement. We need passionate men to pour their life experiences into the starving young men who are confused about faith, culture, and their future.

Young people need encourager (balcony people) who can encourage them to explore the boundaries of what a successful future looks like. Older men need to help young men discover the keys to being a man after God's heart.

WHAT IS GOD TELLING US?

In the First Century, the apostle Paul found himself in a similar dilemma. The culture was corrupt, immoral, and debased with the rich, powerful, and politically connected ruling over the masses. The young church was tempted to avoid being intentional about their faith. Young men were hard-drinking, fast-talking, flippant, unruly, morally lost, and in disobedience to the church.

The apostle Paul found a helpmate with Titus, one of his earliest converts. Titus assisted Paul in Antioch, Corinth, and Ephesus during the third missionary journey. After Paul's release from his first Roman imprisonment (Acts 28), Paul and Titus went to the island of Crete. Paul then commissioned Titus to remain there as his representative. Crete had sunk to a deplorable moral level. The men of this island were well-known for their dishonesty, gluttony, and laziness. By our modern standards they were sluggards or pajama boys.

Paul knew of the lack of spiritual passion, integrity, and commitment among the men. As he pondered his frustration with the
new converts in Crete, Paul penned his letter to Titus to sound
the alarm and wake up the believers to confront the "rebellious
people, mere talkers, and deceivers" found in the villages (Titus
1:10). Paul said, "They must be silenced, because they are ruining
whole households by teaching things they ought not to teach—
and that for the sake of dishonest gain." (Titus 1:11)

Paul tells the men of Crete to look up, measure up, and man up.
Look to God, get your act together and be the biblical leader of
your home. Young men didn't get a pass. Paul realized that if the
younger generation failed, God's Word would die a quick death.
Although he addresses four distinct groups (old men, young men,
old women, young women), Paul was particularly tough on the
younger guys to *Man Up*!

> *You, however, must teach what is appropriate to sound doctrine.*
> *Teach the older men to be temperate, worthy of respect, self-con-*
> *trolled, and sound in faith, in love and in endurance.*
>
> *Likewise, teach the older women to be reverent in the way they*
> *live, not to be slanderers or addicted to much wine, but to teach*
> *what is good. Then they can urge the younger women to love*
> *their husbands and children, to be self-controlled and pure, to be*
> *busy at home, to be kind, and to be subject to their husbands, so*
> *that no one will malign the word of God.*
>
> *Similarly, encourage the young men to be self-controlled. In every-*
> *thing set them an example by doing what is good. In your teaching*
> *show integrity, seriousness and soundness of speech that cannot*

be condemned, so that those who oppose you may be ashamed because they have nothing bad to say about us. (Titus 2:1-8)

Titus was to teach in the congregation *what is in accord with sound doctrine.* This is the idea that certain behavior befits sound doctrine, and other behavior is not a good witness for Christ. The victims of false teachers (Titus 1:16) were out of harmony with sound doctrine; but now Paul would describe the right sorts of behavior.

Paul understood the vulnerability of the younger men. Paul admonishes these young men to grow up—*be self-controlled or sober minded.* He encourages the older men to help push the young guys forward when they want to fall back and pick them up when they fall-down. They can't become manly disciples by themselves. They need godly leaders who can act like men.

Being sober minded speaks of self-control. Self-control addresses immaturity that keeps men glued to video games instead of enjoying them in moderation. It is immaturity that keeps young men obsessed with pornography instead of pursuing a bride in whose beauty he can take delight. It is immaturity that traps men in fear and apathy and keeps them from making bold decisions. Immaturity is a modern-day plague for younger men.[24]

How do we develop self-control? It is a fruit of the Holy Spirit indwelling in us. We need the presence and power of the Holy Spirit that He gives as we discipline ourselves in prayer, meditation, and studying God's Word.

"And if the Spirit of him who raised Jesus from the dead is living in you, he who raised Christ from the dead will also give life to your mortal bodies through his Spirit, who lives in you." (Rom. 8:11) Being filled with the Holy Spirit is how to live a full and dynamic life (Ephesians 5:18).

Undoubtedly, Paul and Titus knew of the words from Proverbs 25:28, "Like a city whose walls are broken through is a person who lacks self-control." In Crete as well as America we need men who practice self-control, a virtue in which many young men are deficient.

Titus qualified as a young man too, and so received some direct advice from the apostle. He must strive to "show himself" an example to all in every good work (cf. 1 Tim. 4:15–16). In his public ministry of teaching, Titus must show an integrity, seriousness, and soundness of speech that cannot be condemned (Titus.2:7–8).

Paul knew that his life and ministry were going to be short-lived, so his encouragement to Titus and the young men on Crete would be key to propelling the ministry forward for future generations. He implied to Titus and Christ's other disciples, "It takes a man, to show a man, how to be a man." While being tough on men Paul also knew that the real strength in being a man is to know where to go with your weakness. It is in Christ we find our strength.

Paul, like King David, could say, "I am about to go the way of all the earth. So be strong, act like a man, and observe what the LORD your God requires: Walk in obedience to him, and keep his decrees and commands, his laws and regulations." (1 Kings 2:2-3)

Queen Mary ascended the throne of England in 1553 after her father King Henry VIII died. Her father had separated the Church of England from the Roman Catholic Church. In subsequent years, Queen Mary was known as "Bloody Mary" because she had at least two hundred people put to death (often by fire) for their religious convictions.

When Mary became Queen of England, she worked to bring England back to the Roman Catholic Church. One of her first acts was to arrest Bishop Ridley, Bishop Latimer, and Archbishop Thomas Cranmer who had become zealot pastors for the Church of England. After serving time in the Tower of London, the three were taken to Oxford in September of 1555 to be examined by the Lord's Commissioner in Oxford's Divinity School.

When Ridley was asked if he believed the pope was heir to the authority of Peter as the foundation of the Church, he replied that the church was not built on any man but on the truth, Peter confessed that Christ was the Son of God. Ridley said he could not honor the pope in Rome since the papacy was seeking its own glory, not the glory of God. Neither Ridley nor Latimer could accept the Roman Catholic mass as a sacrifice of Christ. Latimer told the commissioners, "Christ made one oblation and sacrifice for the sins of the whole world, and that a perfect sacrifice; neither needeth there to be, nor can there be, any other propitiatory sacrifice." These opinions were deeply offensive to Roman Catholic theologians.

Both Ridley and Latimer were burned at the stake in Oxford on this day, October 16, 1555. As he was being tied to the stake, Ridley prayed, "Oh, heavenly Father, I give unto thee most hearty thanks that thou hast called me to be a professor of thee, even unto death. I beseech thee, Lord God, have mercy on this realm of England, and deliver it from all her enemies."

Ridley's brother had brought some gunpowder for the men to place around their necks so death could come more quickly, but Ridley still suffered greatly. With a loud voice Ridley cried, "Into thy hands, O Lord, I commend my spirit...," but the wood was green and burned only Ridley's lower parts without touching his upper body. He was heard to repeatedly call out, "Lord have mercy upon me! I cannot burn. Let the fire come unto me, I cannot burn." One of the bystanders finally brought the flames to the top of the pyre to hasten Ridley's death.

Latimer died much more quickly; as the flames rapidly rose, Latimer encouraged Ridley, "Be of good comfort, Mr. Ridley, and *play the man!* We shall this day light such a candle by God's grace, in England, as I trust never shall be put out."

My friends, God is calling out for each of us to *play the man!* To man up to a world filled with sin and entrapments. Don't be afraid to stand your ground as the attacks come from those who do not see or comprehend God's plan for mankind.

DISCUSSION QUESTIONS:

1. What changes in the culture have you personally witnessed regarding manhood?

2. How would you respond to the oft-repeated question, "Where are the men?"

3. In what ways has the lack of strong male role models affected your life?

4. In what ways has the presence of strong male role models impacted your life?

5. What things can you personally change in order to Man Up and be a strong male role model for others?

CHAPTER FOUR
CHARACTERISTICS OF MANHOOD

It takes a man, to show a man, how to be a man.

Therefore, since we are surrounded by such a great cloud of witnesses, let us throw off everything that hinders and the sin that so easily entangles. And let us run with perseverance the race marked out for us, fixing our eyes on Jesus, the pioneer and perfecter of faith. For the joy set before him he endured the cross, scorning its shame, and sat down at the right hand of the throne of God.
– Hebrews 12:1-2

Unless there is a restoration of biblical manhood, we can ill expect there to be restoration of an ordered society. – Dr. Tony Evans

Eric walked out on the airstrip and performed the pre-flight check on the open cockpit, Ryan PT-22 airplane. Every time he climbed into the quirky plane he was soberly reminded that 110 of the 215 cadets in his class had died in flight training due to the idiosyncrasies of this aircraft. General Hap Arnold would later order significant changes to the design of the plane to make it safer. But Eric knew nothing of that now.

Eric loved to fly and had taken to it naturally. So, on this clear, warm day in Texas, he fired up the Ryan and taxied down the airstrip for takeoff. With permission from the tower, Eric pushed the throttle forward and felt the plane shudder under the rumble of its engine. He released the brakes and began accelerating down the airstrip and the plane lifted lightly into the air.

He loved the speed and the added thrill of flying in the open-air. He gained altitude and prepared to do some acrobatics. He was good at it and had learned how to beat the quirks of this airplane that had claimed so many lives.

Satisfied with his altitude, Eric dove the plane into a spin. This was the very maneuver that had proven fatal to many cadets. He planned to pull out of the spin after three revolutions, but the controls weren't responding to his commands and the plane continued its deadly spiral toward the earth.

Eric tried to remain calm and continued his efforts to pull out of the spin, but to no avail! Six, seven, eight spins with the ground coming ever closer at increasing speed! Beads of sweat appeared on his brow. Every muscle in his body tensed as he focused on bringing the plane out of its deadly spin. He was beginning to get dizzy—not a good sign for maintaining his faculties.

Finally, after what he estimated to be 13 spins, he forced the plane out of its deadly course and leveled off just 50 feet above ground. Shaken, he regained some altitude and cautiously headed back to the airstrip.

He landed the plane without mishap and taxied to its tie-downs. After shutting down the plane, he sat there contemplating what had just happened and breathed a prayer of thanks to God. He climbed out of the plane and removed his headgear. Once again, he went over the whole plane trying to determine why it refused to respond to him. Finding nothing on the outside, he inspected the cockpit again. To his horror, he found a handwritten sign stuffed under the seat. It read, "Do not use this plane for acrobatics!"

The sign that should have been posted in plain sight had been hidden out of view. He placed the sign on the seat and went into the control room to report the mishap. This would not be the last close call Eric had in his stint as a training pilot during WWII.

Eric was born in a small town in Missouri in 1924. He was fourth in the birth order of five children, his siblings all girls. When he was six years old, his father died of influenza, leaving Eric's mother with five children and a large house to care for.

Following the death of Eric's father, his aunt and grandmother came to live with them, making Eric the only male in a household of seven women! One might suspect that all that estrogen would have had a profound feminizing effect on Eric, but this was not the case.

As the only male to continue the family name, the women in Eric's life were all keen to preserve, protect, and nurture Eric's masculinity. As a result, Eric exuded masculinity and virility. Even as a small boy of six, he began contributing to the family financially by selling magazines and newspapers on the city street corners. In high school, he was a star athlete in track events and could high jump his own height of 5'11". His coach urged him to train for the Olympics.

But when WWII broke out, Eric enlisted right after completing high school. Through testing, he was selected to train as a pilot, which meant he had to become an officer. But being an officer required a degree. The Army Air Corp (as it was called then) sent Eric to an accelerated college degree program from which he emerged with a bachelor's degree.

Eric became an excellent pilot and then a flight instructor, due in part to his extraordinary talent for flying. Eric trained hundreds of pilots through the duration of the war.

When Eric returned home after the war, he continued his education by pursuing a unique skill he had inherited and had cultivated for many years. Eric had an amazing baritone voice. Since the age of four, his mother had scraped funds together to send Eric to voice lessons. He had continued exercising this skill into adulthood and now enrolled at the Kansas City Conservatory of Music.

Eric's voice coach claimed that a voice like his only came once in a generation. Soon Eric had his own recordings and a radio program. Through his initiative, he met the famous composer Sigmund Romberg and auditioned for him. Romberg was immediately taken with Eric's voice and commanding stage presence and invited him to be his protégé and move to New York to further his career.

Eric moved his wife and newborn son to New York and began the arduous climb to prominence in the entertainment world, taking whatever jobs he could to provide for his young family. Over the next five years, he worked hard at his profession. He sang in the Metropolitan Opera, hob-knobbed with movie stars, and landed a contract to perform weekly with one of the Gabor sisters.

By now, Eric's family had flourished to include three boys. But one evening, when he returned from work, his wife met him at the door and through tears exclaimed, "Eric, I can't live here anymore." Eric pulled his wife into his arms and tenderly responded, "Alright, Honey, we'll begin to put things in motion to move away from here." But his wife urged, "No, you don't understand. I have to leave now."

It's unclear what brought on her sudden and desperate need to move out of New York. But her fear was so great that she had wired her parents for money, packed up their meager belongings in their furnished apartment and was ready to go.

Eric stood before one of the most significant choices of his life. If he left New York now, he would be walking away from a promising future in the entertainment industry, a career that he had prepared for and invested much in for many years. But as he weighed his career against loving his wife and boys, there was no contest. That very night, Eric packed his family and their belongings into their car and headed for Minneapolis, Minnesota.

Eric sacrificed his musical career and perhaps a chance at stardom in show business for his wife and children. Remarkably, he never expressed regret about his decision, especially to his wife. He never threw his sacrifice back in her face, but only expressed deep love and affection for her. In fact, one could argue that his great sacrifice for his wife only made his love for her that much greater. Often, in public with her on his arm, he would turn to those around him and say, "Isn't she beautiful?"

When Eric's wife contracted terminal cancer, he served as her in-home caregiver. After she passed away, all he could think about was the joy of one day being reunited with his beautiful bride. So, it was fitting when, some years later, Eric too passed away on the 60th anniversary of the day he met his beloved wife.

A CHANGING CULTURE

This story is how most of us from either the GI or Boomer generations remember the roles of a mother and father. Later in this book we will discuss in more depth how the perspectives of our roles have changed.

Ms. Hanna Rosin is a senior editor at *The Atlantic* and author of several books. She wrote an article in *The Atlantic* in 2010 called *The End of Men—How Women are Taking Control of Everything.* This article later developed into a book with the same title. With some authority and good research, she states the case for the decline of manhood and strength of men related to all facets of life. "At this unprecedented moment, women are no longer merely gaining on men; they have pulled decisively ahead by almost every measure."[25]

Similarly, one of the top authorities on raising sons and daughters is Dr. Michael Gurian. From his studies and clinical practice, he indicates that "In most of the world, girls and women are doing better than boys and men in both physical and mental health indicators. Even when statistics regarding female depression, eating disorders, and violence-against-females are included, males are doing worse."[26]

CREATED IN GOD'S IMAGE

While the trend in our world is heading one direction the initial design of our respective roles has been clearly identified in Scripture and by the crafting of our bodies. Psychologically, men typically focus on one primary task at a time, while women are more capable of multi-tasking. (E.g., have you ever watched a mom with a baby in one arm while making supper for her family and conversing with a friend on the phone all at the same time?)

Additionally, men tend to be more adventure-seeking, task-oriented, and risk-takers. Men are usually the "hunter" and women the "nurturer—gatherer." While there are exceptions to and some blending between the genders regarding these psychological characteristics, there are no exceptions when it comes to the biological and physiological makeup of males.

There are unique relational characteristics of manhood as well. Only a man can fill the roles of husband, father, son, brother, uncle, nephew and grandfather. These relational roles too are established by our Creator and help define manhood.

Part of the confusion over gender these days stems from the unhealthy and egotistical focus on individualism. God designed man and woman to complement one another—not to compete with one another. "The Lord God said, 'It is not good for the man to be alone. I will make a helper suitable for him.'" (Genesis 2:18) And, "That is why a man leaves his father and mother and is united to his wife, and they become one flesh." (Genesis 2:24)

For the genders to function properly as God designed us, each gender must fulfill his/her roles and responsibilities. I believe that we can summarize all these distinctive male characteristics and roles with two primary responsibilities: *protector* and *provider*. We see these two male responsibilities in Scripture, and whether we acknowledge it or not, they are innate. As men, we know deep down that we are to protect and provide for those whom God has placed in our care.

God is our heavenly Father. He is our Provider and Protector. One of His names is Jehovah Jireh (the Lord will provide). God is also depicted as our Shepherd who provides us with all we need

(Psalm 23). In that same Psalm, we learn that He is our Protector as well. In fact, the Bible is filled with metaphors that describe these two masculine roles of our heavenly Father. Fatherhood and manhood are inseparable concepts.

In His role as Provider and Protector, God has made great sacrifices for His children (us). In the same way, men are to love their wives and children sacrificially (Ephesians 5:25). God models for men how we are to fulfill our role and He asks us to imitate Him. This is not only implied in the fact that He created us in His image, but we see this elsewhere in Scripture as well. In Ephesians 5:1, Paul urges us to, "Follow God's example."

We find another very sobering element in referring to God as our Father. As humans, we would have no reference for understanding the term "Father" apart from our experience here on earth. So, when God refers to Himself as Father, He is risking His reputation based on our experience and understanding of fatherhood.

I have interviewed women who were sexually abused or otherwise abused by their earthly fathers. The damage their earthly fathers did to them skewed their understanding of God as Father and distorted their concept of men. For many of these women it has taken decades of healing to be able to unlearn the image that their earthly fathers portrayed of fatherhood and manhood.

One of the NT metaphors for the church is that it is the Bride of Christ. This metaphor depicts Christ as husband, and the church as his bride. Addressing the church at Corinth, the apostle Paul referred to himself as the one who gave the church to Christ, presenting her as a pure bride to her one husband (2 Corinthians 11:2–3) Christ protects and provides for the church and a man should do the same for his woman. [27]

Similarly, if we are to love our wives like Christ loves the Church and sacrificed His life for her, then could it be that our love for our wives is testimony to the Church of Christ's great love for them? As I said, this is a sobering but biblical concept. We men bear a huge responsibility.

Let's take a closer look at each of these roles of provider and protector.

MEN AS THE PROVIDER

Most men eventually marry, so we're focusing on our relationship with our wife and children from this perspective. But even if you are unmarried as a man, you are still called to be a provider; it simply means that you will be providing for someone other than a wife and children. And if you are married, you still may be called upon to care for aging parents, a sibling, grandchildren, nephews and nieces, or others who are unrelated to you.

In a man's role as provider, he is to provide:

- Sacrificial love (putting family before self)
- Leadership
- A godly example to follow
- Food

- Shelter

- Finances

- Safety

- Spiritual leadership

- Instruction and discipline for his children

The above list isn't exhaustive, and it doesn't imply that only men can or must provide these things, but all those things fall within the realm of our responsibility as men. However, in this regard, many men have fallen into a narcissistic self-focus that has rendered them lazy, authoritative, foolish, brutish, and even irresponsible by exploiting those for whom they should be providing.

In 2 Timothy 3, Paul warned Timothy:

> *But mark this: There will be terrible times in the last days. People will be lovers of themselves, lovers of money, boastful, proud, abusive, disobedient to their parents, ungrateful, unholy, without love, unforgiving, slanderous, without self-control, brutal, not lovers of the good, treacherous, rash, conceited, lovers of pleasure rather than lovers of God—having a form of godliness but denying its power. Have nothing to do with such people. – 2 Timothy 3:1-5*

As men, our role as provider is so vital to manhood that the Scriptures declare, "But if anyone does not provide for his relatives, and especially for members of his household, he has denied the faith and is worse than an unbeliever." (1 Timothy 5:8 ESV)

Let's look more closely at a couple of the basic things we must provide.

SACRIFICIAL LOVE

Husbands, love your wives, just as Christ loved the church and gave Himself up for her to make her holy, cleansing her by the washing with water through the word, and to present her to Himself as a radiant church, without stain or wrinkle or any other blemish, but holy and blameless. In this same way, husbands ought to love their wives as their own bodies. – Ephesians 5:25-28

Men, we are to love our wives "just as Christ loved the church and gave Himself up for her." Jesus suffered humiliation, false accusations, injustice, torture, being nailed to a cross and hung to die. He did all that out of His great love for us, His church. "For the joy set before Him he endured the cross." (Hebrews 12:2)

The love of a husband toward his wife is sacrificial. But what does that mean? Does it mean that we give her anything and everything her heart desires? Does it mean that she always gets her way as we forfeit ours? Of course not!

Some years ago, a friend of mine was working for a large company as their training manager. Shortly after the events of 911, he and 72 others were downsized due to loss of business. Over the next few months, he threw himself into job hunting. Finally, a large church in Alaska called him and offered him, not one, but his choice of two jobs!

He was elated! He felt honored that this church would offer him a job at all and to give him his pick of two jobs was sheer bliss. He was also excited about the prospect of living in Alaska. For him, this was the fulfillment of a lifelong dream!

But his wife responded to this offer differently. She stated emphatically, "I am not moving to Alaska for either of those two jobs!" He was dumbfounded! How could she say that? He was ashamed to admit that what followed was one of the most heated arguments they'd had in their nearly 30 years of marriage!

In the heat of the moment, he stormed out of the house, slamming the door to punctuate his anger. He went for a walk to process the whole mess. He knew he wasn't acting very lovingly or spiritually. He didn't get very far from home before he heard the Holy Spirit speak to him, "Your wife is right. Go home and apologize to her and trust Me."

So, he walked back home, held his wife in his arms and through tears apologized for his reaction. As they embraced, he told her, "Honey, I want you to know that whatever we do, we're going to do together. So, on Monday, I'll call the church and decline their offers." And with that, peace was restored between them.

When Monday rolled around, he was preparing to call the church in Alaska when his phone rang. It was one of the pastors at that church. His wife was listening in on the conversation as this pastor explained:

> You're going to think we're a bunch of wingnuts up here, but we want to rescind the offers we made to you and replace them with a different offer. You see, over the weekend, the pastoral staff and

elders got together on a retreat to pray about the direction of the church. As we prayed, we sensed the Lord telling us that our focus should be discipleship and leadership development. And we think you're the guy to bring this about. Will you come help us?

My friend couldn't believe his ears! Discipleship and leadership development are his passion. This is what God designed him for. But how would his wife respond?

Immediately, her eyes filled with tears and she said, "That's it. That's the job worth moving to Alaska for." They moved to Alaska and worked at that church for five wonderful years and saw God do some amazing things! My friend praised God that God got through his hard-headedness and worked in a way that enabled him to love his wife sacrificially. And by his willingness to "love her sacrificially," God worked in such a way that the situation was even better than he could have imagined.

Look back at that text from Ephesians, Chapter 5 again. Frequently, I hear men (and women) say that they've become bored with their partner. "She no longer turns me on." "She let herself go." "I'm no longer attracted to her." And so on.

But what we read in Ephesians kills that self-focused mindset. I don't know what church you attend, but let's face it, often the church is anything but lovely. And yet Christ loves her and seeks "to make her holy, cleansing her by the washing through the word, and to present her to Himself as a radiant church, without stain or wrinkle or any other blemish, but holy and blameless. *In the same way, husbands out to love their wives."* (Ephesians 5:26-28 emphasis mine)

Jesus doesn't love us grudgingly because the Father obligated Him to do so. Instead, such gracious, beautiful, sacrificial love springs up from Him because of who He is. As a result, He finds much joy in His bride, the church, despite all her imperfections. Like Eric in the story above, He says of His bride, "Isn't she beautiful?!"

Men, as followers of Jesus, we want to mimic Him. Our goal is to become more and more like Him. And as we do, we will love our wives as He loves the church. We do so willingly and with joy, doing those things that enable us to fall in love with our wives each day afresh.

When we follow Jesus and provide this joyful, sacrificial love for our wives, everything else we're to provide for them falls into place.

OUR ROLE AS PROTECTOR

Unfortunately, our reputation as protector is not a shining one. From the very beginning of time, we men have shied away from our role to protect our wives and others. When Adam and Eve lived in the paradise of the Garden of Eden, the devil came in the form of a serpent and tempted Eve. We know Adam was present, but he was silent. He was passive. He never objected to Satan's devious arguments. He didn't move to stand between Eve and the serpent. He just stood there like a dumb ox (Gen. 3:6).

I don't mean to imply that I'm any better than Adam. I say these things just calling them as we see them and hanging our heads in shame as men who have often forfeited our role as protector. Unfortunately, we see Abraham in this light as well.

The Bible graciously refers to Abraham as "the man of faith." But when he and his wife Sarah visited the region of Gerar, it was not Abraham's finest hour. Apparently, Sarah was so beautiful that he was afraid the King of Gerar would kill him and take Sarah to be his wife. So, Abraham lied about his relationship with Sarah, claiming she was his sister.

But his plan backfired, and the king sent for Sarah and took her into his household. Sarah was placed in a very compromising position because of her husband's fears and feeble attempts to protect himself at the expense of his wife. And were it not for the Lord's providential protection, things could've gotten very ugly for Sarah. (See Genesis 20.)

In this feministic society today, there are too many men standing and watching as Satan perverts our families with mixed messages and confusion about gender, roles, duty, and a host of other devious issues. Many men stand by as their kids flounder with the progressive teachings of educators and leaders who worry more about being politically correct than being sensible or biblically accurate when it comes to issues of manhood.

When we go back to the Garden of Eden and observe where the battle against manhood started, we recognize it for what it is. First, it is Satan's attempt to pervert and destroy what God designed.

Second, it is a battle. But it's not a battle against women, or even against society. It's a battle against the evil one, who wants to destroy, pervert and distort manhood and masculinity.

The question is, will you run from the battle or to it?

"Act like men!" (1 Corinthians 16:13 ESV)

How might we summarize what real Christian Manhood looks like in the 21st Century? Here are ten traits:

1. Real men seek to know God intimately and desire to follow His Word in their words and actions.

2. Real men respect themselves and others (especially women).

3. Real men take on the responsibility to provide for and protect their families.

4. Real men accept the responsibilities that come with their jobs and seek to honor God by being a forthright employee.

5. Real men don't let hobbies, lusts, and temptations distract them from their primary mission in life.

6. Real men seek to be in control of themselves.

7. Real men develop a character that glorifies God and their family. Integrity is a high priority.

8. Real men reject passivity and lead courageously.

9. Real men invest in eternal things.

10. Real men seek to support, encourage, and mentor others. This is an eternal investment that helps make the world a better place.

DISCUSSION QUESTIONS:

1. In studying Genesis 1:26-31; 2:1-25, what stands out about the specific roles God intended for man and woman?

2. How do the Ten Traits of Christian Manhood mentioned above apply to your understanding of biblical manhood?

3. What additional thoughts come to mind about Christian Manhood and how can you better incorporate all these things into your life?

CHAPTER FIVE
HOW MANHOOD IS DEVELOPED

The big question is not whether we function as a role model for others, but how well we do so.

Set an example for the believers in speech, in conduct, in love, in faith and in purity.
– Paul to Timothy in 1 Timothy 4:12

Man was meant to function like a mirror—something to reflect the image of God into creation. –Dr. Eric Mason

If you were to look at Josh's life today, you would see a man of integrity who embodies a godly masculinity that is a tribute to his gender. Josh, who is in his forties, is a follower of Christ. He is in love with his wife, has four beautiful children, holds a prestigious management position in the workplace, is active in his church, and daily living a Spirit-filled life.

But the man you see today in Josh demonstrates how deliberate we must be in the development of manhood.

When Josh was eight, his parents left him at home in the care of two female babysitters. That night they sexually abused this little boy robbing him of his innocence. Subsequent to this traumatizing experience, Josh developed a deep-seated fear of women.

Added to this fear of women, he was confused by the male role models in his life. First, there was his grandfather on his mother's side. His grandfather was the stereotypical macho male. He was a rough, tough Irishman who portrayed masculinity as one who beats up, belittles, and overpowers others. His grandfather was a womanizer and abuser who had multiple wives.

The other prominent role model in Josh's life was his own father who was simply emotionally silent. Josh's dad's demeanor was negatively influenced by his absent father who had taken his own life. Josh's dad wasn't physically absent, but stoically mute. He demonstrated the notion that men don't show emotion. They just act and move forward.

Josh fit neither of these stereotypes and he didn't want to model his life after them. He was a passionate, emotional boy and the poor examples of his father and grandfather confused him and made him feel inadequate. This helped forge his self-image to believe that something was fundamentally wrong with him. His feeling of inadequacy led Josh to believe that he was different in a bad way.

These clashing, unfortunate role models of manhood coupled with the trauma of sexual abuse, led Josh down a path of homosexual experimentation. No longer a minor, at one point, Josh had physical contact with a 17-year-old boy. Deeply repentant over his actions, he went to the one man in his life he knew he could trust, his uncle.

Josh wept as he courageously confessed his sin to his aunt and uncle. His uncle was a man he greatly admired. He was strong and masculine, yet he openly expressed love and affection toward his wife and children—and toward Josh. His uncle also followed Jesus and demonstrated godly character in everything he did.

Josh's uncle listened intently to Josh's confession and then calmly told Josh, "You have to tell your parents, and I'll go stand with you." Josh accepted the decision to own up to his sin and take responsibility for his actions regardless of the consequences. He points to this decision as a turning point in his life that put his feet on the road to manhood and spiritual growth in Christ.

Having owned up to his crime, Josh went to prison, but after serving his sentence, he emerged a new man. He chose to emulate his godly uncle rather than his womanizing grandfather or stoic dad. His marriage to his lovely bride led him further down the path to manhood as he learned what it means to love his wife sacrificially and to provide for and protect her.

Josh and his wife have been blessed with four children, two boys and two girls. Being a father has opened his eyes to his responsibility for demonstrating what a godly man and father looks like for his children.

Following Jesus and portraying a godly example has evaporated the confusion of his youth. With the help of his uncle and some of the principles set forth below, Josh has become a man. Christ has brought healing to his life and made him the man, husband and father that his wife, children and others look up to and respect. Josh takes his role very seriously and intentionally trains his boys to become men as well.

THE "M" WORD

Our culture is on a rampage to eradicate the "M" word—*masculinity*, or *manhood*. But before we get too judgmental about the degradation of our society, consider the following:

Like Josh's grandfather and father in the above story, many men portray a horrible picture of manhood and masculinity. We men are to blame for the warped view of manhood that is so prevalent in our culture today.

- Many fathers have abandoned their families. According to the US Census Bureau, 41% of children in America live absent their biological father.[28]
- Post-abortive women report that 51% of abortions were "forced" on them by a man.[29]
- Men sexually exploit women in the most degrading ways through pornography.
- One in three young girls and one in five young boys are sexually abused before they reach 17, usually by a man.[30]
- In her lifetime, one in six women in America are victims of rape or attempted rape by a man.[31]
- For decades, men exploited women in business by paying them less than their male equivalents and denying them promotions based on their gender rather than their qualifications.

Is it any wonder that our society is fed up with the "M" word if that's what masculinity looks like?

However, its abuse and misrepresentation do not warrant its demise. One could raise similar arguments for obliterating the "F" word—femininity, but that's not the point. We believe there is a righteous, good, and wholesome version of manhood and masculinity that can be cultivated and modeled for the good of all society and the glory of God.

Obviously, this ideal masculinity requires more than the XY chromosome, a beard and a penis. When we speak of biblical masculinity, we're talking about the male expression of God on earth as provider and protector.

MANHOOD IS A CHOICE

As we saw in Josh's story above, the development of biblical manhood doesn't just happen. Developing manhood is a deliberate choice. Its development also requires good role models who mentor and train.

Our culture plays a huge role in how manhood is perceived. Television, ads, magazines, movies, the Internet all contribute largely in defining what it means to be a man. To a great extent, sitcoms of recent decades have portrayed men as lazy, clueless slugs. Perhaps that was funny for a while until we started mimicking what we watched.

Now our culture is telling us that a man can be a woman if he wants to, or a woman a man. We are confusing our children by neutering society. Such thinking defies all common sense, science, psychology and, of course, Scripture.

When we say that manhood is a choice, we don't mean it in the sense that our upside-down culture suggests. What we mean is that producing a godly, masculine character in a male requires a deliberate course of action. What does this look like? Following are some suggestions and strategies for developing masculine character.

GOOD ROLE MODELS

As a child, one of my heroes was Tarzan. Although there have been many actors who played that role over the years, in my opinion and that of many others, none could match the skills of Johnny Weissmuller. He wasn't merely an actor but ranked as perhaps the best competitive swimmer of the 20th century, winning five Olympic medals for the United States and setting over fifty world records.[32]

In the Tarzan movies in which he starred; he often performed the dangerous acrobatic stunts himself.

But what impressed me about Johnny Weissmuller's portrayal of Tarzan went beyond his physical and athletic prowess. On the screen, he was also a man of character. He protected the weak, had a keen sense of justice, was loyal to a fault, he courageously risked his own life to save others, and was a one-woman man (in that role at least).

Granted, it was all make-believe. Tarzan was just fiction in the movies, but that's precisely my point. Those who wrote the screenplays and directed the films chose to portray Tarzan as an ideal man: strong, protective, considerate, respectful, and courageous. Is it any wonder that this little boy wanted to be like him?

As men who follow Jesus Christ, we are called to provide others with godly examples of manhood. Consider the following passages:

I have set you an example that you should do as I have done for you. – Jesus to His disciples in John 13:15

Follow my example, as I follow the example of Christ. – Paul in 1 Corinthians 11:1

Join in following my example, brothers and sisters, and just as you have us as a model, keep your eyes on those who live as we do. – Paul in Philippians 3:17

You became imitators of us and of the Lord… And so, you became a model to all the believers in Macedonia and Achaia. – Paul to the Thessalonians in 1 Thessalonians 1:6-7

Set an example for the believers in speech, in conduct, in love, in faith and in purity. – Paul to Timothy in 1 Timothy 4:12

Encourage the young men to be self-controlled. In everything set them an example by doing what is good. – Paul to Titus in Titus 2:6-7

Now, you might say, "Wait a minute, those verses aren't about manhood, they're about following Christ." You're right but consider the following. Who was the perfect man? Of course, Jesus was. So, doesn't it stand to reason that the more we men become like Jesus, the more manly we will be? No one has ever demonstrated true, God-ordained manhood better than Jesus did. As a man, follow Jesus' example and you'll become more and more a role model for manhood.

Of course, Jesus came to represent all of mankind—men and women alike—and show us all how to pursue God. But it would not be proper to say that Jesus demonstrated true womanhood in the same way He did so with manhood. Instead, Jesus showed men how to treat women. In fact, the way He interacted with women was often controversial and counter to the distorted views of first-century Israel (and of the United States today).

Our culture has made a huge error when we interpret "different" as "inferior." Difference does not imply inequality. We need to learn to celebrate the distinct differences between men and women while maintaining the equality of both.

Note the unique ways we are to view the two genders and their relationship to us in 1 Timothy 5:1-3:

> Never speak harshly to an older man, but appeal to him respect-fully as you would to your own father. Talk to younger men as you would to your own brothers. Treat older women as you would your mother and treat younger women with all purity as you would your own sisters. Take care of any widow who has no one else to care for her. (NLT)

The character qualities expressly and implicitly provided in this text include respect, tenderness, loyalty, deference, kindness, all purity, protection, love and care. And because they were written to a man (Timothy), we identify these character qualities as those of a godly man.

But most of us learn best, not by reading something, but by watching others. As with many skills in life, manhood is more "caught" than "taught." For this reason, we need role models and mentors. We need people who will provide the time and guidance to walk with us through the storms and successes we face in life.

The simple principle behind role models is that we become like those with whom we spend time. Anyone with whom we spend time will influence us in our behaviors and our thinking. The Scriptures demonstrate this principle at both ends of the spectrum:

Walk with the wise and become wise. – Proverbs 13:20

As iron sharpens iron, so one man sharpens another.
– Proverbs 27:17

Do not be misled: "Bad company corrupts good character."
– 1 Corinthians 15:33

One of the best ways to learn what it means to be a real man is to spend time with real men. We need godly role models of manhood in our lives and we need to model manhood to others— and especially to our children. Too many young people are being influenced primarily by gangs, social media, television, violent video games, and unlawful thugs.

My work with various teams in the NFL reminds me of conversations I had with some athletes. In addition to serving as a chaplain, I had the privilege of sharing my thoughts on developing good character. Today, it is mandated by the NFL Commissioner that every team spend time discussing character development.

After one of my talks, I remember a young player coming up to me and saying, "Man, I didn't ask to be a role model. I feel I can do whatever I want." My response was, "By virtue of what you do, who you are, and the God-given abilities you have, you are a role model. And by the way, we serve as role models for others whether we choose to be or not. The big question is not *whether* we function as a role model for others, but *how well* we do so."

MENTORING AND TRAINING

Mentoring and training go together with providing a good role model for others. A godly example provides the credibility and authority upon which mentoring, and training can be built. The "do-as-I-say-not-as-I-do" model does not work!

Also, the kind of mentoring and training we're talking about is highly relational and works best when conducted in the context of real life. Relationships are messy. There's no one way to mentor and train boys into manhood that works for all boys and men.

Manhood and masculinity are transcendent qualities that are independent of personality or gifting. Because of the influence of society, we often associate manhood with specific vocations, hobbies, or actions. However, it doesn't matter whether a man is a doctor or a nurse, a pilot or a flight attendant, a manager or a secretary. Any man in any vocation can exhibit masculine qualities.

Therefore, we said that relationships are messy with respect to mentoring and training. For instance, let's say you are a father and are raising two boys. Perhaps one of them is an outdoorsman and the other more artsy or intellectual. Both boys can become very masculine, but the way they express their manhood may look different for each boy.

Some have misunderstood the Proverb: "Train-up the child in the way he should go even when he is old, he will not depart from it." It is important to remember that we must train and encourage them in the gifts and talents God has given them and not what we hope them to be. If I am an outdoorsman and my sons are gifted in music or computer science, I am not to try to develop them to be Rambo of the woods or the next fishing show host. I must endeavor to discover their natural and spiritual gifting and support the development of their gifting.

HOW WE MENTOR AND TRAIN

Rightly understood, mentoring blends serving as a role model with training. A mentor trains and leads by example. There is no mystery to mentoring. We don't have to view mentoring in the strict mentor/mentee sense. If as a father you are following Jesus and training your sons (and daughters) to do the same, then you are mentoring them.

Sometimes serving simply *as an example* speaks louder than any training we might provide. For instance, how we behave behind the wheel of a car or how we treat our wives is much weightier in the life of our children than telling them how to behave in those circumstances.

On the other hand, there are times when *training and teaching* is fitting and should be a dominant course of action. When our child has made a poor life choice, we want to seize that training moment, talk about decisions and consequences and not let the opportunity slip by.

One of the chief ways we mentor and teach our boys to be men is showing and training them how to treat women. We are to treat women with respect:

- Open the door for a woman
- Let a woman go first
- Protect women
- Speak respectfully about them and to them

The above is especially true of one's wife, mother, sisters, aunts, and grandmothers.

Another way we mentor and train our boys to be men is through the Scriptures. Paul reminds us in 2 Timothy 3:16-17, "All Scripture is breathed out by God and profitable for teaching, for reproof, for correction, and for training in righteousness, that the man of God may be complete, equipped for every good work." (ESV)

We see from that passage that all Scripture is the very breath of God. He is its Author. All Scripture is "profitable," "useful," "beneficial," or "valuable" for "teaching, reproof, for correction, and for training in righteousness." Those activities describe the full range of coaching by a father or mentor.

And finally, we use Scripture to teach, reprove, correct and train, "so that the man of God may be complete [or thoroughly equipped] for every good work."

In addition to the explicit teaching of the Word, the true stories contained in the Bible offer powerful examples of manhood. Following are some of the men of God that we can learn from:

- Abraham – Genesis 12-23

- Jacob – Genesis 25-33

- Joseph – Genesis 37-50

- Moses – Exodus 3-19

- Job – Job 1-42

- Joshua – Joshua 1-24

- Gideon – Judges 6-8

- Samson – Judges 13-16

- Samuel – 1 Samuel 1-7

- Jonathan – 1 Samuel 14

- David – 1 Samuel 16-31; 2 Samuel 11-12 and Psalm 51

- Nehemiah – Nehemiah 1-13

- Jeremiah – Jeremiah 1-52

- Daniel – Daniel 1-6

- Peter – Luke 5:1-11; Matthew 14:22-33; 16:13-27; 26:69-75; John 21; Acts 1-5; 10-12

- Paul – Acts 9; 13-14; 16-28; 2 Corinthians 11:16-33

And there are others as well. As fathers and mentors, we can read one of those stories together with our boys and young men and discuss them using some generic questions:

What was the primary challenge for this man in this story?

- In what ways did he trust God? In what ways did he fail to trust God?

- What mistakes did he make?

- How did he overcome the challenge before him?

- In what ways did this man portray godly masculinity?

- In what ways did this man fail to exhibit godly masculinity?

- In what ways can you identify with the man in this story?

- How did he treat other people through what he experienced?

- In what ways do you want to be like this man?

- What challenge are you currently facing that apply to this story?

- What life lessons can you take away from this story?

- What do you think God wants you to do as a result of reading this story?

In addition to reading and discussing the stories of men of God in the Bible, one of the best ways to mentor and train boys and young men according to 2 Timothy 3:16-17 is to use open-ended questions. Consider the following examples:

- How has God been revealing Himself to you through His Word lately?

- What's one thing you'd like to see Christ change in your character?

- If you were to identify your single greatest struggle, what would it be?

- What has God been doing in your life lately?

- How would you currently describe your relationship with Jesus Christ?

- What has God been teaching you from His Word lately?

- In what ways is Christ using you to represent Him to others?

- In what ways are you leading your wife and children into deeper relationship with Christ?

- How can I pray for you today?

- In what ways are you demonstrating your relationship with Jesus to your mother, sister, grandmother?

Posing a simple, open-ended question like one of those above can prompt a deep, spiritual discussion. We can craft such questions to fit the stage of life of the person we're mentoring. Often, just one question will suffice to get the boy or young man talking. Also, mentoring does not necessarily require a formal arrangement. I often pose questions like those above when I am with men on a hike, meeting in a coffee shop, out fishing, or wherever else we might be.

Yet another way to use Scripture to mentor and train a boy or young man is to systematically read through and discuss short sections of Proverbs 1-7. These seven chapters are all addressed to "my son" or "my sons." Solomon wrote these chapters as instructions for his sons, so they have direct application for mentoring and training boys to be men. By using Scripture, it takes the focus off the specific issue or problem your son is facing so the two of you can address the matter from the position of a third person.

In those chapters, Solomon addresses numerous topics, many of which pose serious temptations for young men. These chapters also serve as a reminder that we need to address with our sons and young men the current "hot" issues of our culture. But it seems that we rarely do this. Some of these issues include:

- Sex and the importance of waiting till marriage.

- The dangers of "fooling around," fondling and caressing a girl before marriage.

- Pornography – what it is, why it's so destructive, how it exploits women.

- Masturbation – the physical, spiritual and sexual dangers of self-gratification.

- God's take on abortion.

- Gender identity confusion.

- What the Bible says about homosexuality.

- How to resist the advances of a seductive woman.

- How to treat a young woman with all purity.

- The difference between love and lust.

- How to find a mate.

- How to stay happily married.

- Guarding your heart and your eyes.

And there are a host of other relevant topics out there worthy of training and discussion.

There is also an enormous side-benefit to serving as a godly role-model and mentor for our sons and other young men. That side-benefit is that by deliberately taking on this role, we become more Christlike ourselves. We become more intentional about living for Christ. We become more careful about our thoughts, our behaviors, and our words.

By helping other young men with their masculinity, we become more masculine.

We've seen that the development of godly manhood cannot be left to chance. We need to take on this challenge deliberately through a variety of means. We also recognize that because Jesus is the perfect man, the more we become like Jesus, the more masculine (in its truest sense) we will become. Additionally:

- We develop manhood in others by deliberately serving as role models.

- We also mentor and train them. Mentoring combines the two vital aspects of serving as a role model and training.

- One of the primary ways we mentor and teach our boys to be men is showing and training them how to treat women.

- Another way we mentor and train boys and young men is through the Scriptures, especially following the model in 2 Timothy 3:16-17.

- We can use the true stories in Scripture to develop manhood in our boys and young men.

- We can also use the plain teaching of the Word and couple that with powerful, open-ended questions.

- We can use Solomon's instructions to his sons in Proverbs 1-7 as a model for addressing contemporary issues affecting manhood in our own culture today.

- Finally, when we serve as role models, mentor and train others, we become more godly and manly ourselves.

DISCUSSION QUESTIONS:

1. In what ways can you relate to Josh's story at the beginning of this chapter?

2. In what ways is pursuing manhood a choice?

3. Who were the most significant positive role models in your life as you were growing up?

4. What are some ways we can mentor and train boys and men to be godly men?

CHAPTER SIX
THE GENERATIONAL GAP

By helping other young men with their masculinity,
we become more masculine.

I go the way of all the earth; be strong, therefore, and prove yourself a
man. And keep the charge of the LORD your God: to walk in His ways,
to keep His statutes, His commandments, His judgments, and His tes-
timonies, as it is written in the Law of Moses, that you may prosper in
all that you do and wherever you turn.
– David to his son, Solomon in 1 Kings 2:1-3 NKJV

Without healthy intergenerational interaction most churches will become isolated and marginalized. – Peter Menconi

Every generation struggles with its own unique sin issues and every generation seems to stand out with its own distinct strengths. But every generation has struggled with manhood since the fall. Just like the ancient kings of Judah and Israel, each generation must decide whether they will follow the Lord, or a god of their own choosing.

Time and time again, we read in 1 and 2 Kings and 1 and 2 Chronicles that a king came into power, "who did not follow the Lord like his father David had." As stated above, no generation is faultless, but our current generation appears to have fallen into a deep spiritual slumber and we're beginning to see the impact of that in our families, in our children, and in society. And once again, this present generation is grappling with the issue of manhood—perhaps to a greater extent than ever before.

In this chapter and the next, I'd like to look briefly at six generations spanning about 100 years to the present. Perhaps we can find our way again if we understand what went right and what went wrong with each successive generation.

In my research I've come across some interesting evidence that might help us better understand some of the significant factors that led to what I call "The Great Disconnect" starting in the early 1990s. American story-teller Louis L'Amour once said, "Much of the study of history is a matter of comparison, of relating what was happening in one area to what was happening elsewhere, and what had happened in the past. To view a period in isolation is to miss whatever message it has to offer."[33]

It is not my intent to offend, judge, or condemn any of the six defined generations discussed in this and the following chapter. Please do not read these chapters with shame or guilt but with the idea that all of us need to work together to mentor those wishing a different life and help build a stronger faith around the principles found in God's Word and our Constitution.

The whole issue with identity: divisive politics, social unrest, bigotry, and victimhood has created a divide that brings out the worst in us. History has shown that if the bedrock of unity and mutual respect is not maintained, then like a cancer to the flesh, our spirit and determination will collapse from within. The apostle Paul addressed the ancient civilization in Rome with the same passion and intensity: "May the God of endurance and encouragement grant you to live in such *harmony with one another*, in accord with Christ Jesus, that together you may with one voice glorify the God and Father of our Lord Jesus Christ." (Romans 15:5-6 ESV *emphasis added*)

To obtain a better understanding of our heritage and why certain generations have a different prospective and worldview from other generations, I would like to trace a few of the traits that shape each generation's approach to dealing with life. The goal is to learn more about those around us and ourselves so we can find a pathway to understanding, respect, and gratitude, that we might find the true essence of manhood.

A HISTORICAL VIEW THAT IMPACTS OUR PERSPECTIVE

The study of modern U.S. History is significant in helping us understand why there is some disconnect between the generations. From the beginning of World War I (1914-1918), the leaders of our nation were strong managers and men of courage. That by itself garnered respect from the citizens of a grateful nation. Gratitude was a trait that was inherent and taught as a family value and shaped our thinking about living in America. It was so powerful that people from all nations sought to come to America to obtain a better life.

In the early 1900s, our country was transitioning from an agrarian culture to becoming a world industrial leader and had its focus on major issues like resolving *The Great Depression* and more global considerations such as world wars. Young people were participating with family in the basics of life so they could survive. The pride and power of unified families was palpable and contrary to people who spoke in selfish terms like "me," "mine," and "my." Teamwork and loyalty were especially significant among family members. There were no televisions, Xboxes, computers, or cell phones that consumed and distracted a person's time and energy.

It was presumed that if you were a young man who was physically fit and determined you would find a way to serve your country. Patriotism was an accepted and respected virtue for all

Americans. Hard work was a core value for the majority. Unless you were physically unable, letting the government take care of you was not an acceptable option.

Following the death of President Franklin D. Roosevelt in 1945, an eager and brash vice president Harry S. Truman stepped into the presidency. Truman had fought in WWI and served for several years after in the Army National Guard. He followed Roosevelt with a passion to utilize his military leadership training to help guide a struggling country and economy back to greatness.

Since President Truman's term as the 33rd President of the United States (1945-1953), our nation has elected patriotic service men who experienced the heartaches, sacrifices, dedication, discipline, and appreciation that comes with defending our democracy. Many were very highly decorated men and some even graduated from our prestigious military academies.

- Harry S. Truman (Army) WWI
- Dwight D. Eisenhower (Army) WWI & WWII
- John F. Kennedy (Navy) WWII
- Lyndon B. Johnson (Navy) WWII
- Richard Nixon (Navy) WWII
- Gerald Ford (Navy) WWII
- Jimmy Carter (Navy) WWII
- Ronald Reagan (Army) WWII
- Gerald Ford (Navy) WWII

- George H. Bush (Navy) WWII

Someone once said, "A true testing of a man's character is to go to war and fight for his country." Except for George W. Bush, who served with distinction in the Air National Guard, Presidents Clinton, Obama, and Trump have not personally experienced the forging of character that war brings to a soul and the appreciation one obtains from serving their country. In 1962, Bill Clinton declared himself a conscientious objector and spent some of his college time hiding out in Oxford, England. I mention this to make the point that when Bill Clinton was elected to be our president, he represented a shift in the focus our culture valued as important and fundamental. His background was politics, not leadership forged over the anvil of life-and-death battlefield decisions or running a major business.

It's also interesting to note that many of our past presidents were Eagle Scouts. Again, leadership that earns respect and embraces self-discipline is something developed in those formative years and helps establish one's mind and heart to a form of patriotism that is different from other leaders.

I'm not suggesting that war is good for the soul and spirit of a young man or that you need to be a decorated war hero to be a good president or leader. It is also not my intent to suggest that any of our recent presidents were not truly patriotic because they didn't serve in the military. However, I believe that great leadership skills, patriotism, and self-sacrifice are developed in circumstances such as serving in the military or managing a successful business. In those situations, people are called to give of themselves for a higher and more noble cause than self, which helps create a character of gratitude, responsibility, and courage. It is contrary to an entitlement mentality that unfortunately marks the nature of many people who inherited wealth, fame, or fortune.

THE WARRIORS WHO SET THE PACE

It's amazing to me that just a century ago, in World War I, seventeen and eighteen-year-old boys were climbing in and out of cold, muddy trenches while enduring toxic gases and constant shelling from the enemy. They were fighting "the war to end all wars" only to return home and face *The Great Depression*. These same young men had to grow up fast and struggled to make a living and develop a legacy for future generations to follow. Their everyday lives were filled with duty, honor, achievement, and courage that gave us the world we enjoy today. We recognize this generation as the **GI Generation** (1906-1924).

The GI Generation embraced individualism and for the most part didn't understand the benefits of teamwork, vision, and big dreams in the same way many of us do. Unfortunately, most women were not valued or respected for the contributions they could make in building a great nation. Most members of the GI Generation held a modern worldview, placing much faith in mankind and its problem-solving ability through science and technology. To some degree their religion was about patriotism that occasionally blinded them to the flaws of our nation at that time.

This was the generation that founded major corporations and international ministries. They developed new suburbs and were the stay-at-home moms who became the grandparents to the Baby Boomer Generation.[34]

They have much wisdom to offer other generations but did not offer it freely. We must probe into their humble lives to hear the stories that created such a powerful spirit within their generation.

Yet, for all its good qualities, we also recognize that this generation gave birth to the Roaring 20s. While this was a period of unprecedented economic growth, it also spawned the consumer mentality, riotous living, and mobsters.

Then came World War II, and we saw the **Silent Generation** (1925-1943), also referred to as The Greatest Generation, head off to yet another war. Over 11% of our male population, or approximately 16 million men, left productive jobs and college classes to serve in the Armed Forces. It was many of these brave troops who fought on two fronts to confront tyranny and evil. Sacrifices were made and some 405,399 Americans were killed in action.

Unfortunately, some of the same men had to fight in a smaller conflict in Korea that lasted for three years where 5.7 million American's served. Today, there are still 2.25 million Korean war veterans alive.

Ever a man's world, the Silent Generation dedicated their lives to the organization or company. Devotion to one's company became a key element of religion. These were the ones of our middle class who left home, spiritually as well as physically, to take the vows of corporate life. They became the mind and soul of our great self-perpetuating institutions. Many of the Silent Generation would have experienced to some degree *The Great Depression* and World War I that shaped their worldview.

Like the previous generation they weren't very open to being vulnerable or communicative. It was believed that if you had personal problems or issues that were impacting your life you just had to "suck it up and stand firm." The expression "Be a Man" back then meant you showed little or no weakness. Unfortunately, that mantra doesn't produce good mental health or much compassion for fellow human beings. They believed their "love language" was being faithful to their job, faithful in marriage, and placing a meal on the table. If you are a real man, then that should be enough. But the reality was that it wasn't enough for the families who lived with this type of leader.

We also note that this generation and its predecessors failed in their attempts to unify the races. Bigotry, racism and segregation were still the rule of the day. Men in this generation also put much stock in unions and secret clubs like the Masons, Shriners, and the Klu Klux Klan.

Some of the children from the Silent Generation fought another war in Southeast Asia called Vietnam. While not a popular war for our country, almost nine million people served in active duty with 47,424 deaths and 153,303 wounded. The senior leadership in the military began to see a decline in, what we call the **Boomer**

Generation's (1944-1962) commitment, focus, resilience, discipline, and morals as our country started to make a turn towards a more liberal approach to parenting, faith, education, and life itself. Some authors suggest that the Boomer Generation didn't start until 1946. And that those born between 1944 and 1946 were called *cuspers* who may show characteristics of two generations. For the purpose of this work I will use 1944 as the beginning of the Boomer Generation that spans a time when over 78 million Boomers exploded onto the American scene.

Failures in our national leadership and the much-protested war in Vietnam changed the worldview of the Boomer Generation. From an early age it became apparent that they were not going to adopt the worldview and values of either the GI Generation or the Silent Generation. Spirituality would no longer be defined by the Judeo-Christian values of preceding generations. Exploration into cults, New Age philosophy, atheism, and self-actualization was part of their divergence from past generations. Hippies, flower children, Spock Generation, TV Generation, and Yuppies exemplified this radically different mindset. A drift from reality and escape from valued norms was a way for this group to thumb their nose at culture.

Generally, this was a happy time for America. The economy was blossoming, technology was evolving, unemployment was low, patriotism was high, police and other first responders were properly respected, and a young President Kennedy inspired a generation towards success through education and hard work. Idealism fueled expectations of young men everywhere. President

Kennedy in his inaugural address on January 20, 1961 challenged the nation, "Ask not what your country can do for you—ask what you can do for your country."

Martin Luther King inspired the nation toward social change that we all are created equal. All Americans could now see a way forward to achieve the "American Dream" of success, education, and respect. The power of media, especially television, would also be involved in social change. At this time most Americans could trust their evening news commentators to be fair and balanced in reporting the news and not trying to create news with fictitious stories.

We could also argue that the sins of the previous generations launched what is known as the Jesus Revolution of the 60s and 70s. Countless churches, Christian ministries, para-church organizations, and mission groups sprang out of that movement. The Jesus Revolution was the last great spiritual awakening that our nation has enjoyed.

In the early 1990s, yet another generation experienced the dread of war. Service men and women of **Generation X** (1963-1981) became involved in Desert Storm and the Gulf War that continues today. More technology and sophisticated battle strategies have lessened the risk among the 694,550 soldiers who were deployed to the theater of war with 1,948 deaths from this action. Many believe the disdain for war and death of young men and women is something our nation can no longer stomach.

Experimentations in how children are educated and fractured families with many fatherless homes created uncertainties and mistrust with this generation. Women began to take on more leadership as strong men were criticized for their leadership at home, in the community, in business, and within the church. Children of this generation have often been spoiled by parents wanting to temper the stress that young people faced by the absence of a father. Many put a higher value on their belief in playtime than their hard work.

More women would be attending and graduating from college than males. Norms had also changed in the workplace for this generation as many men began to slack-off and women were being elevated faster into mid-level management positions.

It seems that many fatherless males struggled with gender identity and what it means to be a protector and provider for their families. Too many males got caught up in fantasies and passions they received from social media and Hollywood. The "fire in the belly for success" that consumed previous generations was not automatically absorbed by this generation. Many believe that the disintegration of family was in part caused by their fathers who spent more time chasing the dollar than being a committed dad and husband. Gen Xers saw educators push for an agenda of changing social values, sexual identity, and liberal positions on everything that they once saw as foundational to their parents' understanding of freedom and family values. The well-publicized failures within the church and the lack of positive male role models led to many guys just riding the wave of peace, status-quo, and entitlement.

The "Sorting Out This Generational Mess" graph put together by Peter Menconi (on the following page) provides a quick insight into the traits that each generation can identify with.[35]

The next two generations show a marked difference from the previous four generations. The following generations would see more change in technology, social status, and global issues than all the previous generations put together. This is a daunting thing to anticipate if men and women entering the job market aren't ready for the myriad of challenges that come with all that responsibility. Women seem to have directly taken the tasks on while many younger men seem content playing with their Xbox games and going with the flow.

We can learn a great deal by studying and listening to the wise counsel of previous generations. Look at the life of one of the greatest men of all time and his words of wisdom to his son. King David didn't want Solomon to fall into the sinful traps he encountered. The great King presented his last instructions to his son before going to glory:

> Now the days of David drew near that he should die, and he charged Solomon his son, saying: "I go the way of all the earth; **be strong, therefore, and prove yourself a man.** And keep the charge of the LORD your God: to walk in His ways, to keep His statutes, His commandments, His judgments, and His testimonies, as it is written in the Law of

	GI Generation 1906-24	Silent Generation 1925-43	Boomer Generation 1944-62	Generation X 1963-81	Millennial Generation 1982-2000	Generation Z 2001-2018
Values	God, Family, and Country	Family, God, Security, Loyalty, Conformity	Competence, Consumerism, Excitement, Non-conformity, Relationships, Family	Self-Reliance, Freedom, Skepticism, Fun and Humor, Friends, Family	Image, Money, Fame, Success, Causes, Social Media, Friends, Family, Mentors	Pragmatism, Social Media, Friends, Entrepreneurial ship, Independence, Mentors
Work Ethic	Work hard, Do whatever it takes, Work is a duty	Work hard, Expect to be rewarded, Work is an obligation	Workaholic, The one with the most toys wins, Work is an adventure	Work to live. Not live to work, Work is a necessary evil	Work should be fun and fast, Work should have a social impact. Work should meet my needs	Work ethic not yet clear, but will probably be harder workers than Millennials
Play Ethic	Work before play	Work until retirement, then play	Work hard, play hard	Play hard, work only if necessary	Play even while working	Probably work and play all the time
Motivators	Sense of duty	Need for respect	Being valued and needed	Freedom for personal time	Flexibility, Social networking	Somewhat motivated by anxiety
Communication Style	Direct, Impersonal	Formal, Guarded	Informal, Face-to-face	Irreverent, Direct and short	Digitally, Constant, Not Face-to-face	Wireless, Constant
Leadership Style	Chain of command	Hierarchical, Titles, Committee	Informal, networks of relationships	Everyone is on their own, Leave me alone	Non-hierarchical, Everyone is equal	Yet unknown
Technology	Radio, Black and white TV, Foreigners to technology	Transistor radio, Color TV, Immigrants to technology	Desktop computers, Walkman, Mostly immigrants to technology	Laptop computers, iPads, Mostly natives to technology	Smartphones, Tablets, Everything wireless, Natives to technology	All wireless technology plus constant change, Always-on restless natives to technology

Moses, that you may prosper in all that you do and wherever you turn; that the Lord *may fulfill His word which He spoke concerning me, saying, 'If your sons take heed to their way, to walk before Me in truth with all their heart and with all their soul,' He said, 'you shall not lack a man on the throne of Israel.'"*
— 1 Kings 2:1-4 NKJV (emphasis added)

In the introduction and first two chapters of this book I described what a man looks like. Let's remind ourselves that strong men are:

- Men who love their wives as Christ loved the church

- Men who long to know God and make Him known

- Guys who respect the rights of others

- As protectors of our families we provide for their needs

- We seek to become positive role models for others to follow

- Men utilize their gifts and talents to help build a vibrant and lasting society

- We aren't led astray by the political and social proponents seeking a politically correct world

- Men seek to be patriotic and respectful of past generations who sacrificed so much

- Guys acknowledge their weaknesses and seek to improve upon their personal relationships

- We remain steadfast and strong in our convictions and work ethic

- We seek the ability to endure major challenges in their fight for survival and freedom

- We are men who desire to leave a testament and legacy to be honored and mimicked by generations that follow.

DISCUSSION QUESTIONS:

1. In your network of family and friends who comes to mind when you think about the GI and Boomer generations?

2. What are the positive qualities from these two generations that can make you a stronger man?

3. How can we live in better harmony with each other (Romans 15:5-6)?

4. In thinking about your impact on future generations how do you respond to this Scripture? "Could it be that God will use people like you and me to help turn the hearts of the children to their fathers and most importantly the hearts of their fathers to their children." (See Luke 1:17.)

CHAPTER SEVEN
PASSING THE BATON TO FUTURE GENERATIONS

As our personal sacrifices to sustain democracy have lessened, the more unappreciative our resolve and attitudes are in upholding the values we once cherished and considered sacred. Simple things like respecting the flag, honoring our veterans, celebrating courage, appreciating the difficult job First Responders have, and embracing faith have become less important in our culture.

My son, if you receive my words,
And treasure my commands within you, ...
...Then you will understand the fear of the Lord,
And find the knowledge of God. – Proverbs 2:1-5 NKJV

As seniors, we must embrace the concept of pouring into the next generation, passing the mantle of leadership, and staying in the race until God calls us home. – Dr. Chuck Stecker

In 1986, the film Top Gun hit the big screen and continues to be an all-time favorite. The film depicts the struggles of a bright young aviator, Pete "Maverick" Mitchell played by Tom Cruise, and a host of other actors who are going through the grueling Top Gun Flight School in San Diego, California. Only the best of the best pilots in the world have an opportunity to receive this advanced training.

During one of the high-risk training sessions chasing A-4 aircrafts, Maverick pressures Iceman (his main competitor for the best pilot award) to break off his engagement so Maverick can shoot down the plane pretending to be the enemy. Maverick's F-14 flies through the jet wash of Iceman's aircraft and suffers a flame-out of both engines, sending his aircraft into an unrecoverable flat spin. Maverick and Goose eject, but Goose hits the jettisoned aircraft canopy head-first and is killed.

Although the board of inquiry clears Maverick of responsibility for Goose's death, he is overcome by guilt, and his flying skill and desire to fly diminishes. The death of his father lost in the Vietnam War was amplified when his friend and co-pilot (RIO – Radar Intercept Officer) Goose died. With no positive way to deal with his emptiness and deep sorrow, Maverick became a loner. He took on the victim role and wanted to quit. His gut response was if he couldn't control it—he would be a loser. By disengaging, he would avoid feeling the pain of defeat and sorrow and find a way to keep his emotions in check.

Like Maverick, some men don't want to experience natural feelings that evolve from loss. They would rather believe that "manning-up" requires either holding those emotions in check or burying them rather than trying to deal with them.

Maverick decided to show up at the graduation party even though he didn't win the Top Pilot Award. He still contemplated quitting. During the ceremony, Maverick and his classmates are ordered to immediately return to *U.S.S. Enterprise* aircraft carrier to deal with a "crisis situation," and to provide air support for the rescue of a stricken ship that had drifted into hostile waters.

Maverick and Merlin (the new RIO) are assigned as back-up for F-14's flown by two other pilots, Iceman and Hollywood, despite Iceman's continued reservations about Maverick's state of mind. The subsequent hostile engagement with six MiG's sees Hollywood shot down leaving Iceman and his RIO to take on six enemies. Maverick's plane is launched alone due to a catapult failure and initially shows up on scene only to retreat after encountering circumstances similar to those that caused Goose's death.

Like many victims of horrendous events, Maverick did not feel equipped at that moment to take on the enemy. He retreated in the same way many men do today—he became a loner wallowing in his self-pity. The Air Boss and Commander back on the *Enterprise* beaconed Maverick to be strong and "get into the fight." He and

Maverick's RIO repeatedly said, *"engage, engage."* Meaning, take action, be brave, do what you are trained to do, act like a man.

After some contemplation Maverick finally rejoined Iceman. Together they shoot down four MiG's and force the other two to flee. Upon their triumphant return to the *Enterprise*, Iceman and Maverick express newfound respect for each other.

The movie so stirred the passions of young men that for many weeks after the film's release, Armed Services Recruiting Posts reported a 45% increase in young men desiring to enlist. Men saw they could contribute despite their fears, brokenness, and past circumstances and make a difference in something bigger than themselves.

Tom Cruise in his role as Maverick displays some of the personality traits and character that many young men face who did not have the profound influence of a biological father in the home or a great mentor in their lives. A person who could help a young man understand that life is not only full of opportunities for those who seek them but has its adversity and failures. Learning to cope with difficult situations is something that is taught and learned through experiencing the disappointments and heartaches life brings.

We do a disservice to young men when we sugar-coat life or protect them against failures and setbacks that are inevitable. Our goal should be to help them learn how to adapt and overcome, and how to trust in God for the power and strength to become victors instead of victims. The writer of Hebrews urges us to, "Endure hardship as discipline; God is treating you as His children. God disciplines us for our good, in order that we may share in His ho-liness. Therefore, strengthen your feeble arms and weak knees." (Hebrews 12:7, 10, 12)

The Millennial Generation (1982-2000) has seen many changes in technology impacting how wars are fought. The present gen-eration of soldiers is more professional in every respect. They are making their mark in history by serving in places like Syria, Afghanistan, Iraq and providing homeland security with the Boomers and Gen Xers.

They are doers and achievers and are very altruistic in their nature. Like Gen X, the Millennial Generation continues to expand its postmodern worldview. They have only known a world that is globalized and diverse. They are well-traveled and appreciate and value a comfortable, non-conflictive world in which to live. When pressed into service they have a tremendous skill set to utilize technology and knowledge to conquer many of the com-plex challenges they face. But many young guys shy away from conflict because it's too painful.

Unfortunately, many of this generation had to face life much like Billy, the little boy mentioned in the Introduction to this book. They were raised in a culture where 50% or more of their gen-eration did not have a father in the home or positive mentor in their lives. Many more competent and skilled women have en-tered the workplace and taken on the tasks men used to do. The traditional strong male icons previously seen in the workplace, movies, television, sporting events, and churches who portrayed positive images of manhood and faith are not very visible or approachable. A softening of America through the feminist movement created more passive men and aggressive women.

As previously eluded to in the July/August 2010 issue of the Atlantic Magazine, Ms. Hanna Rosin, a feminist activist, wrote a well-documented article titled: *The End of Men—How Women are Taking Control of Everything*. In this article she points out a trend that continues to present a challenge to any male not fully engaged in self-improvement.

> *Earlier this year (2010) for the first time in American history the balance of the workforce tipped toward women, who now hold most of the nation's jobs...Women dominate today's colleges and professional schools—for every two men who will receive a B.A. this year, three women will do the same. Of the 15 job categories projected to grow the most in the next decade in the U. S., all but two are occupied primarily by women...According to the Bureau of Labor Statistics, women now hold 51.4 percent of the managerial and professional jobs—up from 26.1 percent in 1980. They make up 54 percent of all accountants and hold about half of all banking and insurance jobs. About a third of America's physicians are now women, as are 45 percent of the associates in law firms.[36]*

I don't have a problem with women being successful. I'm happy for the opportunities they have seized. In a growing economy we will need more professionals at all levels. My issue is with males who have become passive, unmotivated, and who aren't fully engaging in the marketplace. Often, I hear from a woman that her boyfriend, husband, son, or grandson "isn't excited to find a job" or "he has no motivation" or "at twenty-five years of age he still doesn't have a game plan for his life."

WHY AREN'T MANY MALES FULLY ENGAGED?

How does this happen? Again, I will state some of the primary comments from guys I've interviewed:

- "I wasn't prepared to tackle the responsibilities of life without a dedicated father, coach, or mentor in my corner to help guide me with my decisions."

- "The feminist culture and progressive movement has made me feel that if I try to assert myself, I will automatically be presumed a male chauvinist pig, domineering male, guilty of sins other males perpetrated, and a host of other hurtful titles and judgments."

- "Mass-media has redefined and devalued the role and character of males to be the lesser of the sexes. I am tired of fighting the trend."

- "People see mothers as the fixers today instead of fathers. Women see themselves as the leaders of the home and the primary providers in the home."

- "In the past it's been strong men representing a father figure that have led the way to protect and defend the innocence of our children. In America today, there is no one modeling those lofty moral principles."

- "We have become hostages to women who have weaponized their gender to insult and devalue the traits that make up godly manhood."

The apostle Paul urged Timothy, "Don't let anyone look down on you because you are young, but set an example for the believers in speech, in conduct, in love, in faith and in purity." (1 Timothy 4:12)

EMERGING GENERATION

Today, we have a new generation emerging who are professional in every respect. **Generation Z** (2001-?).

Let's hope this generation doesn't have to experience war and can learn from the mistakes of the past. This group will make up a quarter of the U.S. population and by 2020 will account for 40% of all consumers. Understanding them will be critical to companies wanting to succeed in the next decade and beyond.

The recent headline-grabbing studies suggest that Gen Z attention spans have shrunk to eight seconds and that they're unable to focus for extended periods of time.[37]

However, we found that Gen Zers have what we're calling highly evolved "eight-second filters." Mimicking the Millennials, it is a got-to-have-it-now generation where gratitude, hard work, and honoring past generations is not an important value.

SIX DEFINING CHARACTERISTICS OF GENERATION Z

1. They are Cynical

Even though the students I met were happy and well-adjusted, they are not giddy like so many *Generation X kids* were in the 90s.[38]

They tend to be more realistic not idealistic, seemingly jaded from the tough economy, terrorism and complexities of life.

2. They are Private

Perhaps it's because they watched their older siblings get in trouble from posting controversial content on social media, but younger teens don't want to be tracked. Apps like Snapchat and Whisper have seen explosive growth in the last few years. In contrast, Facebook has *lost* 25 percent of this demographic since 2011.[39]

3. They are Entrepreneurial

Like *Millennials*, these students plan to be pioneers, not merely settlers in a career.[40]

72% of current high school students *want* to start a business.[41]

They feel like hackers, not slackers. Since they're more jaded, they know life is hard and requires work.

4. They are Multi-tasking

By almost every measurement so far, these Gen Z kids will take multi-tasking to a new level. They prefer to be on five screens at once, not two screens like Millennials. Get ready to communicate with them while they look around, not into your eyes.

5. They are Hyper-aware

Generation Z has communicated enough with marketing researchers and academics to reveal that they experience 4D Thinking. Because their minds are streaming in so many directions, they've become post-moderns who are hyper-aware of their surroundings.

6. They are Technology-reliant

This one won't surprise you. If we thought Millennials were addicted to technology, get ready for more. In surveys, these teens put technology *in the same category as air and water.*[42]

They cannot imagine living without being connected all the time.[43]

THE CONTRAST

Why would I open the Chapters 6 and 7 tracing the generations by using wars, the military, and a combat movie to setup a discussion of The Generational Gap? Upon studying history and living long enough to know family members from each of these generations, I find some interesting traits that are common to each group, but I also see some distinct differences that are most apparent when you look at the sacrifices they make as young people.

As our personal sacrifices to sustain democracy have lessened, the more unappreciative our resolve and attitudes are in upholding the values we once cherished and considered sacred. Simple things like respecting the flag, honoring our veterans, celebrating courage, appreciating the difficult job First Responders have, and embracing faith have become less important in our culture.

The more progressive and technologically advanced we have become, the less respect and appreciation we have for the personal sacrifices' others have made so we can enjoy life in America. Many just assume that everyone is simply entitled to do what they want with little thought as to the real cost of freedom.

I wanted to set the stage for these chapters with my study of the military, leadership, and generational traits to help us understand the difficulty many previous generations are having connecting and communicating with many young men today. Over the past century we have witnessed a monumental contrast between brave young men going into battle and guys who now only fight fantasy conflicts on an Xbox while lounging in a stuffed chair in their pajama bottoms.

Many are concerned that younger men are whiling away their lives without a plan or a purpose. Life appears to be cheap. The importance of a human life is not valued the same with someone who has seen their friends bleed out on a battlefield verses a Gamer who has just killed a thousand aliens without breaking a sweat. These same pajama boys often hide from conflict and tension because "they don't know how to deal with it," or they buy into the demasculinization of men trend and want a woman to do it for them.

The older generations are trying to understand how so many young people feel they are entitled to something they've neither fought for nor sacrificed for. The GI, Silent, and Early Boomer generations who worked so hard and made many sacrifices for their families are now coping with guilt and shame for "making it too easy" for their children and grandchildren.

Clearly there are very successful and hardworking people among the Gen Xers, Millennials, and Gen Zers. We have many bright and talented young men who are striving to make their mark and have contributed greatly to building a stronger culture. The capable craftsman and blue-collar workers that show up every day to be productive have done their family name proud. And look at all the talented professionals who are keeping the economy growing. They certainly are not Pajama Boys or Snowflakes as some would suggest. So, how did some of our young people get to the place of discontent and lethargy?

TRAITS THAT HAVE IMPACTED THE YOUNGER GENERATIONS

What are some of the issues that may have contributed to those in our younger generation who can't seem to fully engage and commit to a plan for their lives?

- Absence of a biological father or positive role model in the home
- Decreased interest in faith
- Lack of difficult challenges and stress in dealing with tough situations
- The quest for instant gratification—maturity and discipline come with time

- Smaller families, consequently less opportunity for healthy competition
- Over-protective parents take all the risk out of life choices
- Feminization of society has attacked the importance of developing strong men
- A feeling they can't live up to parents' expectations and achievements
- Educational system is geared to under-achievers and a progressive agenda
- Exploration and risk are not part of the culture for most younger men today
- Participants' trophy, no losers, not real-world thinking
- Entitlement mentality—they owe me for just *being* rather than earning the right
- Internet and social media—don't allow for dynamic relationship development
- Lack of physical exercise has created too many unfit and passive men
- Little willingness to volunteer or giving to others on a long-term basis
- Lack of understanding what holiness means—no boundaries or margins—"if it feels good do it"
- Little self-sacrifice—the Great Commandment (Matthew 22:35–40) Love others first

- Shift from an agrarian culture where opportunities for manhood were explored to hi-tech environment without many occasions to dig deep into life and death survival experiences
- More individualism less opportunities for teamwork
- Lack of value for and the sanctity of life—abortion—Xbox (killing games)—violence in videos and television
- Loss of innocence—every kind of immoral sin is now considered justified and accepted
- Hopelessness and lack of positive vision set by leaders
- Fewer mentors who can train others in developing pride of workmanship
- Decline of the Boy Scout movement in the country—youth have little time any more for such things as service organization
- Dot com movement—get-rich-quick role models and schemes minimize patience, hard work, and sacrifice

THE ENEMIES OF OUR CULTURE

In this land of prosperity and abundance, I don't know if we are properly assessing the cultural enemies attacking the church and its men who are supposed to be the spiritual leaders of the home and country. Every day we can observe something in the media and our communities that shows how our culture is moving away from Judeo/Christian values and principles that enabled us to express that we are "one nation under God."

We are now fighting a different war. The battle for decency, morality, and a biblical worldview is not being fought with missiles, bullets, and bombs, yet... but with apathy, wickedness, depravity, and worship of evil. The very sanctity of life with the trend towards taking a fully developed baby and exterminating it is beyond comprehension and all decency. Just two generations ago we wept over the Concentration Camps in Germany that devalued life because people didn't fit into their idea of culture.

We can have disagreements in theology, morality, and politics, but when those who oppose our traditions and faith want to distort reality, re-write history, and devalue others to promote their political and social agendas—then battle lines have been drawn. The battle must be fought by those real men and women who will no longer ride on the wave of a progressive agenda that goes against the Word of God.

My concern is that without a good understanding of past generations and how they viewed life, it will be hard for future generations to follow a set course for life. The reality is that there have always been all kinds of outside interruptions and influences that have stifled the mission of godly men to leave a legacy of great character and faith for future generations.

Are we properly educating, equipping, and motivating younger men to be conquers and victors over evil? Are we losing on the battleground of life for men's souls?

WHAT SEPARATES US?

Dr. Chuck Stecker and Peter Menconi are friends of mine who through A Chosen Generation Ministry do a masterful job in their books *The Intergenerational Church* and *If You Passed the Baton...Take It Back.* They analyze three important questions relative to generations impacting our culture: 1. What events have shaped your generation? 2. How does God speak to your generation? 3. What does your generation have to offer to the kingdom of God? They show us why understanding today's generations is crucial for the survival and growth of local churches. This chapter is insufficient to capture all the pieces and parts impacting our worldview, but their two books do an excellent job viewing the generations.

The chart on the following page will help you quickly see some of the distortions between generations.[44]

It is not my desire to duplicate their efforts but to share some observations that are important for us to contemplate as we try to better understand the complexities and contributions each generation has made to our culture. It is interesting to me that whatever generation we associate with, we don't show enough respect and appreciation to either the generations preceding us or those that come up in our shadow.

While the genre of songs I enjoyed are from the 50's and 60's, I'm amused with the lyrics from the popular 1989 song by Mike and the Mechanics. It goes like this: "Every generation blames the one before. And all of their frustrations come beating on your door."

I just heard of a millennial who wants to sue his parents for giving birth to him. He blames them for his existence and is trying to win a lawsuit for some financial benefit for bringing him into the world. Like, really?! Another person told me that when he confronted his teenager about how much time he spent on the Internet the boy said he only spent the national average of twenty-seven hours a week. The same father walked in on his son a day later watching television and asked his son, "What are you watching?" The son proudly said, "I'm watching some kids doing their gaming on Xbox." Apparently, this young man was so lazy he didn't want to do gaming himself that day but took joy in watching others game.

The fact that people are living longer and being more productive into their 80's and 90's has created a generational phenomenon unique to modern times. The amazing achievements in science and technology can complicate communications and under-standing even more. Today, we can see up to six generations in the same family. Great, great grandad who served in World War II as a seventeen-year-old soldier can see his Gen Z high school graduate enter the service at the same military base where he was stationed in 1940. The World War II vet reflects on a time when a letter took a week to get from San Francisco to New York. The Gen

	GI Generation	Silent Generation	Boomer Generation	Generation X	Millennial Generation	Generation Z
Worship Style	Formal/ Traditional	Traditional/ Predictable	Informal	Eclectic/ Artistic/ Informal	Eclectic/ Informal	Eclectic/ Informal
Worship Music	Traditional hymns	Traditional hymns/ choruses	Contemporary choruses	Newer emergent music	Variety of music styles	Variety of music styles
Preaching/ teaching	Practical	Professional	Relational	Interactive	Integrated	Personal
Community	Family-based	Collegial	Networks of Relationships	Tribes	Global/ social media	Social media
Leadership Style	Chain of Command	Corporate/ committees	Teams	Individualistic	Three dimensional	Four dimensional
Theology/ Faith	Private	Propositional	Practical	Contextual	Global Post-modern	Postmodern/ Post-Christian
View of God	Distant father	Creator and truth-giver	Friend and ally	Compassionate healer	Global connector	Pragmatic helper
Worldview	God is in control of the world	The laws of the universe are at work	The physical, emotional, and spiritual worlds are all related	The world is chaotic and broken	The world can be "fixed"	The world is a dangerous place
Values	Family/ country/ security	Truth/ education/ security	Tolerance/ money/time	Genuineness/ acceptance/ fun	Options/ impact	Opportunity
Work ethic	Do whatever it takes	Stable work/ loyalty/ longevity	Work hard/ play hard/ meaningful work	Work to play/ frequent job changes	Work should be fun and have impact/ Work should meet my needs	More pragmatic about work
Relationship	More formal and positional	Congenial with sense of propriety	Informal and competitive	Individualistic, private, tribal	Digital, social media driven	Wireless Relationships Social media
Needs	Acceptance, care and camaraderie	Inclusion/ stability and safety in the midst of chaos	Sense of purpose and opportunities to "change the world"	Sense of belonging/ opportunities to "heal"	Intergenerational acceptance/ opportunities for impact	Mentors

Z child can converse in real time with someone halfway around the world in milliseconds.

The differences, images, worldviews, and lifestyles that exist among the generations can create barriers that distract us from building unity between the generations. I enjoy watching the very popular television program *Blue Bloods*. It is great to see a four-generational family sit down to have a meal together without cellphones, iPads, and televisions taking people's attention from open and honest communications. Their family is just like each of ours—occasionally fractured, distinctively strong personalities, and sporadically some harsh words are spoken. Yet, despite age differences, mutual respect and love always win-out. Differences and considerations are worked out over a shared meal where everyone has a voice.

Henry Reagan (Pops) played by **Len Cariou** is Commissioner Frank Reagan's father. He is an "old school," City-of-New-York cop who was raised in the 1920s and 1930s. While he is retired from the police department, he is still a valuable member of the family. The Reagan's don't believe you pass the baton of life along to the next generation and assume you're finished running the race.

We have much to learn from those who walked the mile ahead of us and for those who are following our path. Author D. B. Harrop said, "Have a big enough heart to love unconditionally, and a broad enough mind to embrace the differences that make each of us unique."

In the Bible, we see that generations have always been important to God and building His Kingdom. In Genesis 17:7, we read, "I will establish my covenant as an everlasting covenant between me and you and your descendants after you for the generations to come, to be your God and the God of your descendants after you."

Please don't miss the opportunity to appreciate the past generations for all their contributions while encouraging the younger generations to know God more fully and make Him known. If you are older, then you need to engage in mentoring and guiding younger generations. If you are younger, then contemplate what it means to fully engage and plan a life that can be a testimony to future generations. As the apostle Paul admonished the passive disciples of his day, "Awake, you who sleep, arise from the dead, and Christ will give you light." (Ephesians 5:14 NKJV)

DISCUSSION QUESTIONS:

1. What are the implications of the following verse as to how you can impact future generations? "He decreed statutes for Jacob and established the law in Israel, which he commanded our forefathers to teach their children, so the next generation would know them even the children yet to be born, and they in turn would tell their children." (Psalm 78:5-6)

2. What are the contrasts and comparisons you can see in each of the six generations that impact your life?

3. The writer of Hebrews urges us to, "Endure hardship as discipline; God is treating you as His children. God disciplines us for our good, in order that we may share in His holiness. Therefore, strengthen your feeble arms and weak knees." (Hebrews 12:7, 10, 12) What are the hardships you are enduring? How can you apply God's Word to your situation?

4. Who can you lean into for guidance and mentoring? Find another like-minded man and start meeting together weekly.

CHAPTER EIGHT

THE MENTORS WHO SHAPE A LIFE

*We can too easily be consumed with the myth that **being** important rather than **doing** what is important is the focus we should have about living a successful life.*

Follow my example, as I follow the example of Christ.
– 1 Corinthians 11:1

Discipleship is the process God uses to conform us into the likeness of His Son. Our response to the Holy Spirit's convicting and convincing voice is our gift back to a loving Father. – The Spiritual Mentor

Dr. Michael Gurian of the Gurian Clinic and Institute has spent over thirty years as a counselor, researcher, and leader in the field of behavioral science and has contributed greatly to understanding young boys and men. I appreciate the resources he has created to help all of us get a better grip on what is appropriate in trying to communicate with the younger generations.

In this PC (politically correct) environment we hesitate to challenge people with tough words at critical times. Gurian suggest that expressions like, "Let's put on our big boy pants and tackle the problem," should not be offensive and helps bring people back to the basics. In his book, *Saving our Sons,* he also dispels the theory that tough words are damaging to a young man's growing-up experience. He suggests that men who are under-motivated, are *less* likely to bond with a spouse and offspring and be productive in our society.

Simply put, there are times when we just need to challenge a male with frank statements. A question put to Gurian speaks for itself:

Question: Is it good or bad to tell boys, "Be a man!"

Answer: It is generally good to do so because it motivates and matures a boy.

In most cases when people (both women and men) tell boys to be a man, they mean:

- Grow up, stop acting like a kid.
- Stop thinking the world will tailor itself to little old you.
- Be strong, others need you, go help them— it's your duty.
- When you fall, get back up—you're a model for others.
- Don't whine—act with honor and integrity.
- Don't expect the world to give you anything— *earn your success.*
- Take care of the people who depend on you.
- Be responsible and compassionate.
- Be protective and caring, not cruel and heartless.
- Cry when you must, laugh a lot, especially at your-self, and forgive others their faults.

"Be a man" motivates and matures boys because in most cases the comment is warranted: the male is acting in an immature way and needs to be reminded and motivated to grow up to healthy manhood. Certainly, "Be a man!" can be misused. Some people who want boys to show no feelings at all will say it, and this is not the context we are describing.[45]

INFLUENCERS FOR LIFE

Throughout this book you will read about the importance of having positive, influential people in your life and the lives of those you love. Mentors and people with great character can help shape the perspective future generations have about life. Positive role models can represent hope and assurance to those shaping their identity in Christ and pondering how they can contribute to society.

I challenge you right now to take a full minute to think about the men who had the most significant positive impact on your life. These are men who modeled a Christ-like life; who loved and cherished their wives; who were great leaders of their families; who worked hard to make their mark; and who encouraged others in their giftedness. I call these guys Influencers or Spiritual Mentors.

Who did you remember? In what ways did they impact you?

Men have been affected by many factors that have distorted their values, self-worth, and faith. Most churches have failed to connect, train, empower, and deploy men as Christ did with His original disciples. Detached men and the radical women's liberation movement increased the chaos by urging women to take over many leadership positions within the church. Today, there is a lack of biblical male role models for men to follow. Men tend to be loners and lack the support and encouragement that healthy male friendships bring to a relationship. Many of the men left in the church have become spectators leading undisciplined lives instead of active participants in partnership with the Holy Spirit by studying and applying God's Word.

INTENTIONAL LEADER

What is an *intentional leader*? As witnessed throughout Scripture (e.g. Luke 22:7–13; Matt. 14:28–31; John 6:5–6; Luke 10:1), Christ was an intentional leader. Jesus was purposeful in His relationships, and often involved Himself in the daily lives of others. He developed teams, created plans, directed His men, challenged others to address risks and faith, and allowed people to fail. Yet, He was there to assist them, and He met people where they were. Christ's methods, teaching, and training were divinely guided to make the most of His time with others. He helped motivate and move people along in their spiritual journeys.

If we are to be intentional leaders discipling others, we need to care enough to relate on a personal level with those whom God puts in our path. This will require that we deliberately invest ourselves in the lives of others. We need to take time and effort to get to know them intimately, look for ways that we can strengthen them and challenge them, and spend time with them one-on-one or in groups teaching them from God's Word. But above all else, the intentional leader is also a man who deliberately practices what he preaches, who strives daily to live in obedience to the commands of Christ.

THE SPIRITUAL MENTOR

As God put upon my heart to write the book *The Spiritual Mentor* (Thomas Nelson Publishers 2013), several new concepts evolved about this subject. In previous books I had written about building godly character and discipleship. I utilized many of the modern-day concepts about how we go about discipling (mentoring) others. As *The Spiritual Mentor* evolved, I was directed back to the words of Christ and how His disciples applied the principles in establishing the First Century Church.

In my mind, there is a biblical distinction between a person who mentors someone and a Spiritual Mentor or true discipler of others. The Oxford English Dictionary defines a *mentor* as "an experienced and trusted advisor or guide; a teacher or tutor." Secular mentors often focus on social areas such as, work, hobbies, education, and sports to build relationships with others and help them hone their skills in those areas. A mentor in a sense becomes a trusted adviser, counselor, teacher, and guide to someone. Typically, a mentor is a more mature person than the person being mentored.

I define a Spiritual Mentor as a person who disciples another person through deep personal relationship. Being a Spiritual Mentor is ultimately about building a relationship that can help a person grow in their faith. Spiritual Mentorship can also be mutual and reciprocal as both parties become stronger in their faith when there is commonality of spiritual growth. If we agree that the most precious of gifts is *time*, then the idea of investing in others or having someone invest in you is a special gift.

We know from God's Word that it is His design that every Christian be a disciple-maker for Jesus. And the church's responsibility is to equip, motivate, and deploy its members in serving our Lord as disciple-makers. As Jesus was an intentional leader, so every pastor, elder, men's leader, dad, mom, small group leader, and friend of an unsaved person is also a person of influence—an intentional leader. Thus, we all have the responsibility for being an intentional Spiritual Mentor. We lead by example, seeking to apply the Word of God in our daily living. Intentional disciples buy into the process of developing disciples using Christ's modeling, and value a team approach (the church) to reaching others.

An intentional disciple knows the spirit and gifting of those he works with (Ephesians 4:11–13). Some readers will say, "I'm not educated and trained as an intentional Spiritual Mentor." But Spiritual Mentors are men who come from all walks of life. They are men who have an interest in seeing others come to Christ. Being intentional about our approach to the process will require preparation on our part.

We can't model what we don't know; hence, a good understanding of God's Word is important to our ability to be transparent, supportive, and real with those we meet. We strive to adopt a biblical worldview in order to teach others the same. Spiritual Mentors are guided by the Holy Spirit to understand where a person is in his spiritual journey. Are the people whom God has put in your path dead to spiritual things, new in the faith, young in their understanding of God's Word, or seeking to dig deeper into knowing God and making Him known?

In the purest sense, discipling a person requires that you be focused upon the spiritual development of an individual. Discipling a person is helping that person become Christlike in his motives, attitudes, and daily living. Pat Morley provides a good working definition in his book *Pastoring Men*: "A disciple is someone *called* to live 'in' Christ, *equipped* to live 'like' Christ, and *sent* to live 'for' Christ." Thus, a discipler is a person who will help equip the disciple to become more like Christ so he in turn can disciple others.

Pastor David Jeremiah had a great observation: "When you visualize the word *disciple*, what comes to mind? Do you see twelve men in sandals trudging through Galilee with Jesus? Or do you see a church like yours filled with people with open Bibles in their hands? By any chance, do you ever see the person in the mirror? ... *Lifelong commitment, lifelong learning, lifelong service—that's discipleship.*" [46]

Mentoring and discipleship are very similar, and you will find in this chapter that I use the terms interchangeably; however, the essence of discipleship is finding a *Spiritual Mentor* with whom you can connect. The term *Spiritual Mentoring* implies discipling another person within the context of a relational mentoring environment. That is to say, the most effective and long-lasting discipling relationships happen when you seek to encourage and equip the person in areas beyond just the spiritual aspects of life. If you can find common interest areas, such as sports, hobbies, cultural interests, work, or family, your relationship will have dimensions that will help hold you together during trying times. Jesus wants to transform the whole person, not merely their "spiritual life."

During the time of Christ, a spiritual teacher or mentor was called *didaskalos* (or teacher) (Luke 2:46; Acts 5:34). Jewish teachers taught using a discipleship process, allowing the students to ask questions to which the teacher would reply. They did not have any official position and received no salary. These mentors were common men who cared enough about others to share their lives and experiences to help others deal with life.

MY REGRETS AND GOD'S PROTECTION

Early in our sons' lives I was consumed with *trying to be important rather than do what is important*. My workaholic nature, creative personality, and good college education drove me to climb the ladder of success from the inner-city struggles of my youth and threats that marked my growing-up years.

I was determined to be recognized and to provide for my family in such a way that they wouldn't have to struggle like I did. As a thirteen-year-old kid in high school, our financial situation forced me to get a job. The job would ultimately provide me with the funds to attend college and help pull myself out of the mire of a challenging city life.

My parents grew up during the Great Depression and both came from very dysfunctional families. Consequently, their compliments and tangible support were in short supply and my unique skill set and personality posed its challenges for parents struggling with their own identities. Therefore, I was determined to find role models who were successful and could coach me into greatness. Who could fill the void in my life of low self-esteem?

I wanted so desperately to Man Up but sought out some influencers who could only see success in terms of trampling on others or promoting themselves. These role models initially drew me away from my faith and my family responsibilities of being a good husband and father first. For seven years, I too often put my family *after* my job: teaching part-time as a college professor, pursuing the black bass tournament circuit, working sports shows, co-hosting a fishing television show, serving on four boards of directors, writing for outdoor magazines, and all the while trying to grow in my faith.

In 1978 my wife and I attended a parenting conference featuring the renowned Christian psychologist Dr. James Dobson that change my priorities and life. A few months after the conference we attended a family camp with Dr. Chuck Swindoll who modeled, as a speaker, friend, and eventual mentor, what Christian manhood really looks like. My supervisor at my first full-time job was a great Christian man who greatly influenced my choices and helped shape my faith. He didn't judge me but helped me cope with the complicated issues I was facing with my job, faith, and family. All these mentors changed my life and moved my heart towards the things of the Lord.

Seeing how important mentors became in my life I knew that I needed to place good mentors in our sons' lives.

ROLE MODELS FOR YOUNG MEN

As I consider the importance of positive role models (Spiritual Mentors or what could be called Influencers), I need go no further than to share a story about the formative years of our twin sons and the men that have invested in their lives. These friends of mine supported our parenting style, love of Christ, and underscored the values my wife and I endeavored to model for our children. I deeply appreciate those who shared their time and talents in helping our sons become the godly men they are today.

Clearly, their gracious, loving mother had an enormous impact on their lives. Her patience, kindness, and pleasant approach etched into the boys some great qualities. By the modeling she received from her mother, my wife is a wonderful example of a strong Proverbs-31 woman. She is an inspirational and successful person, but desires to be loved, protected, and provided for by a man who desires to lead, guide, and encourage his wife.

Not all of us have the privilege and opportunity to introduce our young people to celebrities or athletes. It is not only the rich, powerful, famous, and important people who can contribute to helping us "train-up our children." Frankly, often the most influential people are those who live a very common life and can connect with people at a basic level. Scouting also played an important part of shaping their love for God's creation and developing leadership skills.

WON'T YOU BE MY NEIGHBOR?

Our boys enjoyed powerful role models of what it means to Man Up: strong military personalities, professional athletes, television personalities, a few pastors, professional fishermen, and even learned professors and scholars from academia.

But during those seven years when I was basically an absentee father, one of the top influencers on our sons was an unlikely man. This man instilled the spirit of love, kindness, gentleness, and grace into my young boys. Hopefully, their grandfathers, a few other Christian men, and I provided some major influence. But without a doubt, one of the key men in their young lives was a tender-hearted guy called Mr. Rogers.

There are those who suggest that Mr. Rogers had some conspiracy to take away manhood and bring on a generation of entitled young people because he suggested that children should accept themselves as they are and that there is no need to work hard or progress from their childish ways. This is wrong thinking and reporting.

Mr. Rogers wasn't projecting that children should have an entitlement or narcissistic attitude or philosophy of life. No, his message was fundamental to the Christian faith: "You shall love your neighbor as yourself. Love does no harm to a neighbor; therefore, love *is* the fulfillment of the law." (Romans 13:9-10 NKJV) His message projected that love and respect can be shared with others. He taught us through his interaction with

Officer Clemmons that there is an appropriate way to handle anger and times when we are mad.

Mr. Rogers gave young children a voice. Through the eyes of a child, he helped us see the good and bad that life brings. It took some of the fear away from those children who were being confronted with issues like the divorce of their parents, death of a loved one, acceptance of people who look different than the average child, and how a sense of peace and joy helps build a better world. Too many children daily face a world where violence and despair are personally experienced in their neighborhood and on the television news. It is loud, scary stuff for children to process.

In their early years, Mr. Rogers came on the TV to inspire and encourage our young lads just before I got home from work. No matter what was going on in their world they would stop the perpetual motion that comes with active twins to tell their mother, "Mom, it's time for Mr. Rogers."

What was it about Mr. Rogers that made him so great to an entire generation who watched him? What is it we can learn from this great man's life that can help us Man Up?

Mr. Rogers was a gifted communicator and minister who truly understood God's love for mankind. He projected that love to his audience. I remember him saying, "Knowing that we can be loved exactly as we are gives us all the best opportunity for growing into the healthiest of people." He really gave hope to those who felt disenfranchised or disappointed with themselves. His message of hope and assurance was important for young people to hear. The thought that as children of God we don't have to earn our way into Heaven or be a sensational person to feel the love of our Creator is affirming to all of us.

Fred McFeely Rogers (March 20, 1928 – February 27, 2003) was known as the creator, composer, producer, head writer, show-runner and host of the preschool television series *Mister Rogers' Neighborhood* (1968–2001). The show featured Rogers' kind, neighborly persona, which nurtured his connection to the audience. Rogers would end each program by telling his viewers, "You've made this day a special day, by just you being you. There's no person in the whole world like you; and I like you just the way you are."

He created a unique learning environment for children. His kindness and gentleness are still greatly appreciated today with two-time Oscar winning Tom Hanks playing Mr. Rogers in the movie, *A Beautiful Day in the Neighborhood* (2019). A special documentary developed in 2018 called, *Won't You be My Neighbor* talked about how Fred McFeely demonstrated his love for mankind by even respecting his gay, black neighbor.

Mr. Rogers' persona had as much or more to do with our sons' mentoring as big strong NFL linemen, successful business leaders, influential political leaders, and a host of other very strong personalities they experienced.

Man Up! Act Like Men–Be Strong includes having the love and respect for others that can accept individual differences while becoming a strong leader. Everyone deserves to be loved. The capacity to receive and give love doesn't make us a sissy. It is something endowed to us by our Creator who loved us so much He gave us His only begotten son, Christ Jesus. We should exhibit that kind of tenderness and love for others today.

In this study, let's not forget what our Savior gave us as a standard to follow even with people who don't agree with us:

> *"You shall love the Lord your God with all your heart, with all your soul, and with all your mind." This is the first and great commandment. And the second is like it:" You* **shall love your neighbor as yourself."**
>
> Matt. 22:37-39 NKJV *(Emphasis added)*

We should all seek to bring back the sense of innocence, wonder, and respect that godly men can teach to the younger generation. Hopefully, this walk down memory lane demonstrates the importance of godly mentors in developing the character and passions of young men.

Think about the kind of people influencing your children. Embrace those friendships with other men who can underscore the values you are trying to project to your children.

DISCUSSION QUESTIONS:

1. What was your childhood like? List the names of those men who helped provide the positive guidance that was critical in your decision-making. If you didn't have many positive influencers in your life, what can you do to break with that pattern?

2. How can you help influence someone in your network by being a positive role model? Notice, I didn't say you need to be perfect. We are all broken and have failed. Sometimes confessing our own brokenness is what can help others along the way.

3. What do 2 Timothy 2:15, Proverbs 22:1, and Psalm 7:8 tell us about the role models we select to follow?

4. In the Sermon on the Mount Jesus spoke a great deal about character. What does His message tell you about how we live a life of godly character (Matt. 5)?

CHAPTER NINE
PUTTING JOY AND HOPE IN
OUR LIVES

Please, Lord, take everything I am, everything I have, everything I value. Take my business, my title, whatever my success, my little material wealth. Take all the respect I've tried to gain. I want to trade it all in—just to know You. – Chuck's prayer

Whom have I in heaven but you?
  And earth has nothing I desire besides you.
My flesh and my heart may fail,
  but God is the strength of my heart
  and my portion forever. – Psalm 73:25-26

For God has not given us a spirit of fear, but of power and of love and of a sound mind. – 2 Timothy 1:7

THE SPIRIT OF GOD

Most men at one time or another desired to be *that* guy. You know, the person with a great family, a good career, all the money you desire to afford most of the neat toys, and the physical assets that set you apart from others. My friend Chuck epitomizes what many perceive as the American Dream Guy. He married a beautiful woman and worked on finishing college in his early twenties.

In 1963, Chuck was dipping into the limited funds set aside for his college and living expenses. A friend asked him if he'd like to purchase his small vacuum business for $2,000. His friend had supported himself through college with this business.

This tiny vacuum repair business consisted of some well-worn equipment, a rusty 1952 Chevy panel truck, and a monthly income of $600. Chuck turned his friend down at first, but when his dad offered to loan him the money, he decided to buy the company.

From the beginning, Chuck and his wife saw this business just to make ends meet. At the time, Chuck had no passion for cleaning, didn't see it as a career option, and had never really considered owning a business.

But with a strong work ethic and a head for business and leadership, Chuck's business began to blossom. By 1970, he had helped friends launch another five vacuum repair companies. That's when he decided to franchise his company and took on the title of "president." Over the next three years, they sold 16 franchises and his business was flourishing.

By 1973, just ten years into this fledgling business, Chuck had it made financially. He, his lovely wife, and three children enjoyed a beautiful home on secluded acreage. He had his pick of cars and could replace them at whim. His lavish income allowed him to pursue his passions of big game hunting and fishing at an extreme level. He and his family were also active in their church.

Admittedly, from the outside looking in, Chuck had it made. He portrayed a happy, successful, self-assured businessman who had everything he needed or wanted. But Chuck confesses that he was utterly miserable. Deep inside, he knew he was living a lie. He had no peace or real joy in his life.

The stresses of the business were weighing heavily on him. The bigger his company grew, the more stress he took on. He felt he was constantly under scrutiny by clients. A customer complaint would expose him to fears and anxieties he had never known. He lost confidence in himself and developed a mortal fear of losing his business, even though it was going so well.

Chuck says that in those days he was "driven by an unholy trinity of success, money, and respect." This pushed him to pursue more money, more success, and more security. But no matter what he did, he found himself becoming more and more resentful and angry. He could never do enough. He was constantly uptight and tense. Even the hint of a problem or complaint would send his stomach into a knot. There was little joy and peace in his life.

Those who were closest to him knew and experienced the real Chuck. None of his toys or their new home satisfied him. At home, Chuck verbally abused his wife and children, constantly chiding them for the tiniest infractions. He confesses, "One stain on the carpet or dead spot in the lawn could ruin my whole day, and therefore, theirs." Everyone around him fell short of his expectations, making him very difficult to live with.

Chuck found himself plagued by irrational fears for his business, clients, employees, finances, and security. "I chewed my fingernails to the quick as I struggled with the stress of maintaining my facade." He also feared whether he was good enough to be saved. If he were to die, would he go to Heaven?

He made multiple trips to the doctor to try to ease his pain. His doctor warned him to slow down and relax or he'd get an ulcer. On his third visit, his doctor prescribed the tranquilizer Valium. He told Chuck to take them as needed but not to exceed three per day. Only days later, Chuck was popping up to six a day to numb his pain and anxiety. He quickly found himself in a downward spiral.

During all this, in the spring of 1973, Chuck's mom called him to let him know that his cousin John was dying of cancer. Chuck and John were the same age and had been very close as children and news of John's impending death hit Chuck very hard. He and John were only 32. How could his cousin die at 32? What would happen to John's wife and two kids? All this led Chuck to consider his own mortality—with fear and trepidation.

Chuck wanted to do something for his cousin and remembered that he loved Gospel music. So, Chuck asked two of his musical friends to go with him to Santa Cruz to sing for John. But when Chuck boarded the plane, he was terrified. He had always suffered from an inordinate fear of flying. He would psych himself up to get on the plane, sit stock-still, grip the seat arms with white knuckles, and flinch with every hint of turbulence. He feared the plane would go down. If he died, would he go to heaven? Even though his dad was a preacher and he'd grown up in the church, he didn't know for sure.

When Chuck saw John in the hospital, he was utterly shocked at his physical condition. The cancer had ravished his body. John was able to speak and was coherent, but he was extremely frail with the pallor of death. But John looked content and at peace with his condition. And as Chuck witnessed John's peaceful composure with his wife and two children, Chuck became undone.

Chuck thought, *"John has more peace in dying than I have in living!"* Lying there looking so pitiful in his cotton hospital gown with IVs coming out of his arms, Chuck realized that John had everything Chuck wanted—without having any of what Chuck possessed.

And there, at the foot of John's hospital bed, Chuck bowed his head and prayed silently:

Lord, the life I've been living is too heavy and painful to live any more. I am desperate to know You and to experience the peace John has found in You. Please, Lord, take everything I am, everything I have, everything I value. Take my business, my title, whatever my success, my little material wealth. Take all the respect I've tried to gain. I want to trade it all in—just to know You.

That prayer was different than any prayer Chuck had ever prayed and now *he* was different. He could feel it. Until now, he had always just tried to "add more God" to the other gods in his life. Now he desperately wanted to know God above anything else.

When Chuck got on the plane to go home, he discovered he was no longer afraid of dying. He found himself totally at ease during the flight home. He now had a peace that he had never known.

Today, Chuck and his wife have helped launch dozens of franchises in 20 states and Christ has continued to transform his life in every area as Chuck has submitted to His leadership.

In recent years, Chuck has decided to leave his children and grandchildren a legacy of five freedoms. He sees these "freedoms" like the heap of stones that the Israelites placed at the Jordan river when God parted it for them to cross on dry ground (Joshua 4:6-7). That heap of stones would remind generations to come of the goodness and provision of God and the peace and joy only an intimate relationship with the living God can provide.

CHUCK'S FIVE "STONES" ARE:

1. "The world's success, excitement, and 'fun' pale in comparison to the joy and fulfillment that comes from truly knowing the Lord."

2. "The 'Christian life' is not a formula or something God expects us to do but is the supernatural 'heart surgery' He continues to perform as we earnestly seek to know Him."

3. "We cannot imagine how good God is. Anyone willing to trust Him with everything will live in awe of all He does."

4. "God is the essence of all that is practical. Whether it's something in the past, a problem today, or fear about tomorrow, believing exactly what God's Word says (no ifs, ands, or buts) brings clear direction and inner peace to every circumstance."

5. "My value and acceptability to God is based totally on what He has done for me, not on anything I could ever do for Him."

"Therefore, if anyone is in Christ, he is a new creation; old things have passed away; behold, all things have become new." (2 Corinthians 5:17, NKJV)

Chuck's story and the five "stones" he has placed on the shore as a witness of God's working in his life, keenly apply to manhood. Whether we realize it or not, it's not the unholy trinity of success, money, and respect that men truly long for, but the peace and ultimate joy found in a relationship with God and knowing His character.

Becoming fully dedicated to Christ doesn't mean we are void of problems, calamities, and significant trials. I know Chuck well and can testify that he has endured some major physical and mental challenges with people very close to him. Having Christ in our lives allows us to endure the trials that life brings with an inner peace knowing that whatever God has allowed into our lives we can trust that He will be there to help us through it. The Apostle Paul had a great perspective on trials: "Therefore, since we have been made right in God's sight by faith, we have peace." (Romans 5:1 NLT)

ON BECOMING A MAN

Throughout the ages and in nearly every culture, people have recognized and celebrated the transition from boyhood to manhood. But for the most part, we have either abandoned this rite of passage or have forgotten how to do this or even how important this is. As a result, not all adult males earn the title of *Men* or even understand what it really takes to be a Man.

As we stated earlier, true manhood is a choice involving a deliberate mindset and resulting actions. We also mentioned that Jesus Christ is our supreme role model and mentor. He is the perfect man. If you want to pursue genuine manhood, follow Jesus and become like Him. As Chuck discovered, this is not knowing more *about* God, but knowing Him at a personal level.

Jesus is the perfect man. The only route to true manhood is to follow Him. To embrace true masculinity, we must aspire to be more like Jesus. How do we do that? It's not by doing things for God but embracing what He has done for us. We do this by following Jesus as His disciples. The way to manhood is through discipleship to Jesus.

Many think that Jesus' disciples 2000 years ago enjoyed a great advantage unavailable to us today. The Twelve disciples spent time with Jesus every day. They saw His life, heard His voice, and witnessed His works. They spent time with Him hiking the breadth and length of Israel. They spent hours in a boat together, fished together, ate meals with each other, experienced His prayers, saw His miracles, and heard Him preach to the crowds. There were also all those private lessons they received when they were alone with Him.

We think about all those many hours spent in Jesus' presence and we may consider ourselves disadvantaged because we don't have those same opportunities. We may even be tempted to think that our so-called disadvantage excuses our half-hearted discipleship.

THE HOLY SPIRIT

But consider this. On the night Jesus was betrayed, He told His disciples, "Very truly I tell you, it is for your good that I am going away. Unless I go away, the Advocate will not come to you; but if I go, I will send Him to you." (John 16:7) When He said this, Jesus was speaking about the Holy Spirit who indwells all followers of

Jesus. And from Jesus' prayer in John 17:20, His promise of the Holy Spirit applies as much to us today as it did to the Twelve back then.

It's vital that we believe Jesus when He said, "It is for your good [or to your advantage] that I am going away." The presence of Jesus within us *by His Spirit*, is a far greater, more powerful, more peaceful, more visceral presence than what was possible when Jesus was here in flesh and blood. No matter when or where we live, if we know Jesus, we are men in whom God's Spirit dwells! Think of that!

Chuck was much like the Apostle Peter. Peter is a great example of the difference we're trying to portray here when Jesus sent His Holy Spirit to indwell us. If you look at Peter's life when he was physically with Jesus, Peter was impetuous, reckless, and wishy-washy. Even after walking with Jesus through His whole ministry, Jesus warned Peter that he would betray Him that very night. I can imagine Jesus saying to Peter, *you are so impulsive and intense you are missing the joy and peace only I can bring.*

But after Jesus' resurrection and ascension, when the Holy Spirit came and indwelt Peter, he became a totally different man! That same day, we see him preaching Christ to the very people who crucified Him. And he did so with boldness, unafraid of the consequences. He was now willing to go to prison and even die for Jesus, which he later did. With the Holy Spirit dwelling in him, Peter began *acting like a man* with the joy of His Lord in his heart.

That is the kind of transformation that occurred with my good friend Chuck. The same power to overcome our human nature is available to all of us.

Jesus told us that His going would be *to our advantage* because of the coming of the Holy Spirit. But we don't take that truth to heart. We seldom live as though God is indwelling us. We don't live *in* His presence and *with* His presence. We seem not to realize the power we can appropriate. The peace and joy that follows our decision to experience the fullness of relationship with the living God, Christ Jesus gives to us. How would your life look if each believer were conscious of Jesus' presence with you 24/7? His Holy Spirit lives, dwells, abides within us always. He gives us the peace and joy we long for.

For this reason, we must learn to listen for and hear the Spirit's voice. Let Him show you how to live. Think, speak, and live in the knowledge of His presence and power within you. If there are things in your life that you know don't please Him, ask for His help in delivering you from those things. Yield to Him. Trust Him. Let Him transform you. Let Him make a man out of you!

We must "walk in the Spirit," "be led by the Spirit," "live in the Spirit," and "keep in step with the Spirit." (See Galatians 5:13-26.) To do so means freedom, love, joy, peace, etc.

Just as Chuck devoted himself to God's Word and his relationship with Christ, the following truths will play a huge role in our becoming more like Jesus and putting on manhood.

THE WORD

Jesus so identifies with Scripture that He is the Word of God. So, it makes sense that God's Word and His Spirit work in unison. "All Scripture is God-breathed." (2 Timothy 3:16) And, "Above all, you must realize that no prophecy in Scripture ever came from the prophet's own understanding, or from human initiative. No, those prophets were moved by the Holy Spirit, and they spoke from God." (2 Peter 1:20-21 NLT) God's Word has been given to us by His Spirit.

Therefore, as you become more and more acquainted with God's Word, it will become easier to discern the voice of the Holy Spirit in your life. But when I talk about knowing God's Word, I'm not talking about just knowing facts. I've met men who know the Bible forward and backward and yet they're arrogant, mean-spirited, and ungodly. Chuck admits that this was his problem prior to really knowing God.

I too once lived flippantly by the saying, "A chapter a day keeps the devil away." We shouldn't read, study, or listen to God's Word treating it like some good-luck charm or religious activity. Instead, when we go to the Word, we must always go with the intent to meet with our Lord. We want to get to know Him better. We need to know His presence, person, peace, and power. That assurance will bring us much joy.

I strongly encourage you to set aside time daily to read God's Word. But do so with a humble and open heart. Meet with God there and let Him speak to you. And as He does, let Him change you.

When you read the Bible, here are some simple prayers you might pray:

- "Lord, what are you saying to me here?"
- "Father, I don't understand what this means. Please reveal it to me."
- "Lord, how do you want me to live my life differently today as a result of reading Your Word?"

There are times when reading His Word will convict you of sin, prompting confession and repentance. At other times, you'll want to praise God with all your strength, as King David did. Often, you'll simply bow in humble adoration, thanking Him for His great love, mercy and grace. Use God's Word to get to know Him.

YOUR BROTHERS

Jesus doesn't call men into discipleship alone. We make a grave mistake if we think we can grow in Christ and into manhood on our own without the help of others. In the story above, the peace and contentment that his cousin John exuded on his deathbed, profoundly impacted Chuck. My regular meeting with people like Chuck has helped hold me accountable and has influenced my life.

When Jesus called the Twelve, He not only called them to Himself but to each other. They learned so much from each other as well as from Jesus.

You cannot possibly grow as a disciple of Jesus and into manhood without the example of, mentoring, and interaction with other men who know Jesus. Both the discipleship process and the path to manhood are highly relational involving other godly men. Often the best mentors are men who themselves have experienced a *masculine wound* of some kind. Men who know of failure, fatherlessness, hurt, pain, suffering, and disenfranchisement can help young men forge a positive plan to conquer their issues.

The Apostle Paul demonstrates the necessity of gathering other brothers around us. Men who have the freedom to speak into our lives. Men who serve as role models and examples to us. Men who can mentor us. Men with whom we can work and fellowship. I devoted an entire book to this subject titled *The Spiritual Mentor.*

If you read Acts, you'll find that one of the only times Paul was ever alone was in Athens for a short time. And he couldn't wait for his co-workers to arrive! He valued their company greatly. Read the final verses of any of Paul's letters and you'll see how much he depended on and valued other Christian men in his life.

One of the chief complaints I have with some churches is they believe all that is needed comes from a pulpit on Sunday morning. Not true. The principles of discipleship are key to any successful church.

The Scriptures offer evidence of the power of pursuing Christ in the company of other men throughout its pages. Consider these few examples:

- "As iron sharpens iron, so one man sharpens another." (Proverbs 27:17)

- "Walk with the wise and become wise, for a companion of fools suffers harm." (Proverbs 13:20)

- "Two are better than one, because they have a good return for their labor: If either of them falls down, one can help the other up. But pity anyone who falls and has no one to help them up." (Ecclesiastes 4:9-10)

- "Do not be misled: 'Bad company corrupts good character.'" (1 Corinthians 15:33)

- "You therefore, my son, be strong in the grace that is in Christ Jesus. And the things that you have heard from me among many witnesses, commit these to faithful men who will be able to teach others also." (2 Timothy 2:1-2 NKJV)

- "And let us consider how we may spur one another on toward love and good deeds, not giving up meeting together, as some are in the habit of doing, but encouraging one another—and all the more as you see the Day approaching." (Hebrews 10:24-25)

DISCUSSION QUESTIONS:

God created us to be in relationship with others. God uses these relationships to help mold and hone us into men. If you don't currently have a relationship with another godly man like I'm describing, I urge you to do so. Here are some helpful guidelines for finding and meeting with a godly confidant:

1. Prayerfully find a man whom you respect for his faith and walk with Jesus and ask him if he would be willing to meet with you regularly (weekly would be best).

2. When you meet, talk about what God is doing in your lives. Be honest and transparent with each other. Discuss God's Word. Pray with and for each other. You may find these questions helpful as you meet:

    • What has God been doing in your life this week?

    • In what ways are you leading your wife and children (or others) into deeper relationship with Christ?

    • What's one thing you would like to see Christ change in your life?

    • Where are you struggling right now?

    • How can I pray for you?

3. Spend time together in real life. You may choose to meet regularly in a coffee shop, at work, in your home, or on a walk or hike together. Get out into situations where you see each other with your families, behind the wheel of a car, and in all kinds of other situations. Much of life's discipleship occurs simply in real life situations. After all, that's how Jesus did it.

In addition to the above tips, look for another younger man whom you can influence for Christ. Serve as his mentor and example of manhood and what it means to be a true follower of Jesus Christ.

CHAPTER TEN
MAN UP!

Christianity without the living Christ is inevitably Christianity without discipleship, and Christianity without discipleship is always Christianity without Christ.
– Dietrich Bonhoeffer

But you will receive power when the Holy Spirit comes upon you. And you will be my witnesses, telling people about me everywhere—in Jerusalem, throughout Judea, in Samaria, and to the ends of the earth.
– Acts 1:8 NLT

*In a common world, an uncommon man is committed to helping others
get to a better place, to giving a hand up to provide opportunities that
could assist others, to using the gifts God has given him and looking
beyond himself to make a difference.* Coach Tony Dungy

New Yorkers are normally known for their edgy personalities
and tough spirits. Some people would even say they can be cold
and brazen on a regular basis. I guess if we lived in a multi-cul-
tural environment where 8.6 million people were crammed into
302 square miles, we too would be a little cantankerous at times.

As eclectic and diverse as New Yorkers can be, time and time
again when the chips are down, the New Yorkers rise to the oc-
casion. Such was the case on 911 when over 500,000 people were
evacuated in nine hours from the seawalls, streets, docks, and
buildings next to the New York waterway.

Shortly after the 911 tragedy hundreds of thousands of shocked
and injured citizens looked for a way to escape the carnage and
damage from the buildings that fell after the two jets struck the
Twin Towers. The bridges had been shut down as a precautionary
step to mitigate any potential terrorism activity so the only way
off Manhattan Island was by boat or helicopter.

Initially, the Coast Guard thought they would be able to handle
the evacuation, but the sheer number of people jumping into the
water to be rescued overwhelmed the limited number of boats
dispatched. The call soon went out as a "May-day" for any boat in

the area to respond. Thousands of civilian boaters made their way to the impact area to transfer people to safer locations.

Most of the rescuers had no formal training or experience to address the actions they would have to take that day. All they knew was that America was under attack and their fellow citizens needed some help. They simply did what they could do.

There is a strength in togetherness when people face the same crisis. A hero is a person who does what he can for another person in their time of need. There were many heroes that day who stepped up and took on the challenges that had limited solutions.

When we measure the actions of these heroic rescuers against history, we find that the next largest evacuation was from the beaches and harbors at Dunkirk in Northern France at the beginning of World War II. This major evacuation came to be known as "Operation Miracle of Dunkirk" or "Dynamo." Over 198,229 Brits and 139,997 Frenchmen were rescued by many military and civilian boaters who risked their lives for the sake of others. It took nine days to empty the beaches of the Allied Forces. Several men died on the beaches waiting to be evacuated.

THE TIME IS NOW!

How the people of New York responded to the 911 Tragedy is indicative of how Christians need to respond to the threats and attacks against the fundamental values of our faith. As the boat-lift rescuers assisted the victims of 911 one life at a time, so it is with the church today. We need to quickly and intentionally reach out to the lost—one life at a time. That is what Christ commanded us when He challenged His disciples to "make disciples".

As we have analyzed the plight of men today there is plenty of blame to go around. Some overindulgent parents from previous generations must assume some of the responsibility for young people's feelings of entitlement. The unrealistic self-assessments and expectations of many young people have been propagated by a pop culture that glorifies and edifies the achievements of athletes, movie stars, performers, and other celebrities. One must only take a quick look at all the role models in reality television shows and many commercials to realize that the icons being promoted by a progressive agenda are fake ambassadors of what is needed to attain and build a life that contributes to society.

Unfortunately, there are too many young men lost on the beaches of uninvolvement, complacency, and pain who have dropped-out or disconnected from an environment that demands effort and excellence from its future leaders. If the younger generation is to make their contributions to building the gateway into the future, they need to embrace the value of developing leadership skills, taking risks, and mastering technology to serve us rather than serving it.

As David Kinneman stated in his outstanding work, *You Lost Me,* "Today the influences of technology, pop culture, media, entertainment, science, and an increasingly secular society are intensifying between the generations."[47]

Starting with the parents from the GI and Boomer Generations we placed a great deal of value on education and worldly success. Those things are important, but not at the expense of forsaking the value of modeling and teaching the significance of forming a personal doctrine of faith and great character. Many have stepped back from an intentional parenting environment believing that the successful and safe environment they created would be enough to develop competent young adults. Also, the increase in marital separation became a reality for too many couples. Parents of these generations may have allowed culture to have to large a role in defining the morality and faith many young people have embraced.

In part, this has become a reality because young people seem to lack the mentoring and nurturing that takes place in a relationship with older, wiser, and more experienced adults. It's hard to get that relationship in homes that lack a positive male role model to assist young men into manhood.

RESTORING THE CHURCH IS A START

If ever we are going to restore biblical manhood, we need to revisit the current plan the church has about how disciples are made. We cannot mass-produce the discipleship experience. It is not an assembly-line process. Authentic disciples are people who have been spiritually mentored by someone who has helped equip, encourage, and transform them into the likeness of Christ Jesus. It seems that too many Christian leaders have leveraged men to build church buildings and run church programs but have failed to disciple them in what it means to be about building the Kingdom.

In order to compete with cultural influences too many churches have placed a great deal of emphasis on BIG events. Big concerts, big churches, big gatherings, and big personalities to drive these events have become the norm. It seems that with all the smoke machines, strobe lights, and pastors with holes in their jeans, wearing Hawaiian shirts and flip flops, we forgot one of the basics of Christianity. When you study the life of Christ, His approach to discipleship was a life-on-life apprenticeship and mentoring experience.

"We need new architects to design interconnected approaches to faith transference. We need new ecosystems of spiritual and vocational apprenticeship that can support deeper relationships and more vibrant faith formation."[48]

With over 80% of our young people dropping out of church after high school graduation it is obvious to me that the "feel good—entertainment approach" to many youth programs needs to be dumped. We need to exchange that for a back-to-the-basics approach to knowing and applying God's Word to everyday living.

This trend has especially hit the male participant. I believe we are one generation away from Christian men being an extinct species in the Christian church. Most European churches are void of any significant male presence in churches. Research shows that with the feminization of the church beginning in the 16th century we started to lose male participation. One-on-one discipleship was no longer seen as a responsibility of godly men, but of the church, a committed mother who regularly attended church, or Christian educational institutions.

In an effort to be P.C., many church leaders have stripped men of their manhood while attempting to encourage themselves by building church attendance from gathering more women into the church who have the passion and time to run committees that control the leadership.

Dr. Tony Evans has a humorous but sad observation:

> *Men feel they are unable to be the men they know they need to be (leaders in churches) and therefore they try to live vicariously through others. One of the primary ways they do this is through sports. They become fanatics...men who will wear another man's jersey with another man's name and number on the back of it. Any man who must ware another man's name on the back of his shirt may need to ask himself how he views his own manhood.*[49]

Tony makes a couple of other observations that expose some of the myths of men being engaged in the church:

- Some men view church like a prostate exam, something that can save your life but is so unpleasant and invasive that they put it off for another day.

- The feeling many men have about attending church is the same as when they hold their wife's purse—something just doesn't seem manly about church.[50]

True male reformers seek to overcome the risks of criticism or cultural influence to embrace the importance of teaching the younger generation about holiness, obedience, and discipleship. They so align themselves with God's plan and a Kingdom agenda the others are benefited and encouraged. The seduction of mainstream influences through mass media, Internet, and dominant ego-driven personalities have pushed the younger generation towards a godless culture that distorts and contradicts the values other generations used to frame their lives and behaviors that built a great nation.

If we are to save our nation, our churches, and our families we must rediscover Christ's teachings on what it means to "go make disciples" (Matt. 28, Matt 4:19). Success in achieving this goal should not be measured by the numbers of people renewing their faith, but the depth of faith and commitment each person achieves as they embrace God's Word and the relationship of a godly mentor in their lives.

Pastors need to rethink current trends on how we teach, preach, and model evangelism and discipleship. It should no longer be about making new members that stay for a month or two but making true disciples who are committed to the life and vibrancy of the church. Discipleship helps men overcome the illegitimate influences and definitions of manhood that society wishes to place on all men. It helps put the joy back in life as we build positive male bonding opportunities.

Many contemporary pastors believe a successful church is about "the show." How much information and production can be displayed in an hour service that produces good attendance seems to be the goal of some. Unfortunately, growing in wisdom and truth are rarely promoted as part of the more contemporary service. Opportunities to teach young boys about biblical manhood are less visible in our post-modern church culture.

SO, WHY IS DISCIPLESHIP SO IMPORTANT?

Why are discipleship and mentoring so important? What place does it have in our faith? How does discipleship connect to men and the struggles they are facing today? On any given Sunday in most churches across America, men will make up less than 39 percent of the congregation. In Europe, the male makeup of the congregation is much worse, around five percent. The most disturbing news suggests that as many as 90 percent of the boys who are being raised in the church will abandon it by their eighteenth birthday. Many of these boys will never return to their faith.[51]

For those precious few who stay in the church, most believe that discipling others is the responsibility of paid professionals—the pastors and missionaries. When we consider the former patriots of the Christian faith, warriors and ambassadors like the Apostles Peter or Paul come to mind. After considering world leaders in the discipleship movement like Martin Luther, John Wesley, Charles Finney, A. W. Tozer, Dietrich Bonhoeffer, Charles Spurgeon, Dwight

Moody, and Billy Graham, today there seems to be precious few whose primary focus is on discipleship or mentoring.

We have many articulate communicators whose Sunday messages inspire people to feel good about themselves, but few are the pastors who preach powerful messages on discipleship that move people to action and to fully commit themselves to the principles of what I call Spiritual Mentoring. There are some twenty-first-century pastors, teachers, and leaders who consistently speak on and model biblical truths about the primary focus of our faith—discipleship—but their voices are being drowned out amidst the idle chatter of liberal theology and "feel good" religion.

We need to revisit what it means to be a true disciple. We need a fresh look at what Christ taught about discipleship. In today's vernacular, first-century discipleship would best be described as Spiritual Mentoring. You will have to visit my book *The Spiritual Mentor* to get a more in-depth explanation of this concept.

Discipleship is a relational process that requires people to become actively involved with others in their faith. It is the men who will lead their families back to faith. It is men who can help save the Christian church from the challenges that other religions are placing on our culture. Devoted and active men are the ones who can passionately change the direction of our culture and its destructive patterns that are leading us into chaos and despair. And, most importantly, God has commanded men to be the leaders in the home, church, and community. Consequently, men do not know who they are as men. Rather, they define themselves by what they do, who they know, or by what they own.

I would agree with that statement, and add that men also define themselves by tasking, duties, and performance. Even when it comes to faith issues, men seem to see their observance of religion by the money they give, the time or work they provide, and by the quantity of Scripture they know, instead of a yielded heart given to God.

There is nothing more fundamental to the Christian faith and to building godly men than discipleship. If our mission doesn't include the ingredient of "helping men know God and make Him known," then we have lost the cornerstone of our faith. Is there a greater mission? Once a man intimately knows God through a divine personal relationship with Jesus Christ, then he is directed to "make Him known." Look at some of Christ's final words to His disciples: "All authority has been given to Me in heaven and on earth. *Go therefore and make disciples of all the nations*, baptizing them in the name of the Father and of the Son and of the Holy Spirit, teaching them to observe all things that I have commanded you; and lo, I am with you always, even to the end of the age." (Matt. 28:18–20 NKJV, emphasis added).

Theologian Dietrich Bonhoeffer said:

> *When Christ calls a man, he bids him come and die. Discipleship means adherence to Christ, and, because Christ is the object of that adherence, it must take the form of discipleship. Christianity without the living Christ is inevitably Christianity without*

discipleship, and Christianity without discipleship is always
Christianity without Christ. Discipleship is ". . . bondage to Jesus
Christ alone, completely breaking through every program, every
ideal, every set of laws. No other significance is possible, since
Jesus is the only significance. Besides Jesus, nothing has signifi-
cance. He alone matters."[52]

Discipling a man needs to be intentional. In some ways it is like driving a car. Guys can pick-up quickly on the skill needed to shift gears, steer in a straight line, brake when necessary, and how to peel out from a stop sign, while looking in control the entire time. But what they initially lack is the wisdom and patience to know to check the blind spots around the car that could cause a problem if they are changing lanes or reversing direction.

Men can't change what they don't see. They need godly men (reformers) to help them understand where their blind spots are and how to correct them. Men don't know what they don't know. One of the purposes of the church is to patiently show men biblical truth and how to practically connect it to daily living. They need blueprints and godly role models that help them understand what godly manhood looks like.

- Recurrent themes in Scripture direct us to discipleship. Here are just a few examples:

- Matthew 5:16, "Let your light so shine before men, that they may see your good works and glorify your Father in heaven."

- Acts 1:8, "You will receive power when the Holy Spirit comes on you. And you will be My witnesses, first here in Jerusalem, then beyond to Judea and Samaria, and finally to the farthest places on earth." (The Voice).

- 1 Timothy 2:3–4, "For this is good and acceptable in the sight of God our Savior, who desires all men to be saved and to come to the knowledge of the truth."

- Romans 10:13–14, "Because *as Scripture says,* 'Everyone who calls on the name of the Lord will be saved.' How can people invoke His name when they do not believe? How can they believe in Him when they have not heard? How can they hear if there is no one proclaiming Him?" (The Voice).

- Romans 1:16, "For I am not ashamed of the gospel of Christ, for it is the power of God to salvation for everyone who believes, for the Jew first and also for the Greek."

- Mark 16:15, "Go out into the world and share the good news with all of creation." (The Voice).

This chapter intentionally directs the reader to explore and define the topic of discipleship and to make decisions about involvement in this crucial aspect of Christianity. Discipleship is more than attending church on Sunday, writing a check to some missionary, or reading God's Word. Discipleship is much more than communicating information about specific topics. All these things are important, but authentic discipleship is about developing a caring concern and a genuine love for others through modeling Christlike attitudes and behavior in the context of relational environments. We must have a clear biblical definition of discipleship and obey God's commands and plan for our lives within that context.

Biblical discipleship requires a believer to get out of the box of traditional thinking and seek new ways to communicate God's Word and love to a culture that has become hostile to things of the Lord. We need a fresh approach to defining, implementing, and equipping others with a passion to *go make disciples.*

WE NEED REVOLUTIONARIES!

If there is any significant hope in America for the Christian faith, it is with pastors and leaders willing to become true Revolutionaries. According to George Barna, Revolutionaries are "people who are devout followers of Jesus Christ who are serious about their faith, who are constantly worshipping and interacting with God, and whose lives are centered in their belief in Christ."[53]

I would add that a revolution cannot occur without true transformation. Revolution requires individuals who so identify with our Master that they become transformed (changed, altered), and who are seeking a walk with Jesus that sets them apart from the culture. These are the ones who will change our world for the better. If enough men pursue Christ to transform their lives, a revival will occur. America has experienced revival before, but it was limited to denominations or specific areas of the country.

If we truly are in the last days before Christ's return, then a global revival will precede His coming. There will be a renewal of our commitment to Christ. Restoration of lives will begin to happen. God will be returned to His rightful place in our society and the people "will turn from their wicked ways." When revival occurs, a Christian Revolution can happen.

Because it all starts with the individual, we must see one-on-one discipleship as the primary objective to begin the Revolution. Within the nature of a man is the desire to win battles, identify with important causes, protect his loved ones, and take on hefty goals that are bigger than life itself. The appeal to Christ's followers in the first century was that many men realized it was an "all in" commitment to be a Christian.

There is no quick fix to the problems of our nation and the decline of interest in the Christian faith. Like a newborn baby, discipling is a life process that begins with care, nurturing, love, and commitment to the responsibilities of being a parent of that child. It requires tremendous dedication, devotion, commitment, and resources to equip a child to be successful in life. So it is with being a true disciple of Jesus. Christ desires each of us to be strong men of character and discipline utilizing the same approach to disciple-making that a good parent brings to raising a child.

As never before, we need capable, strong men of God to disciple their kids and to become the spiritual leaders within their families, churches, and communities. As we have said, "As goes the husband or father, so goes the family, church, or government." Again, it starts with relationship. Mentoring, discipling, and modeling cannot be replaced with governmental mandates or a social gospel.

And it all starts with you. This book is about challenging you to dig deeper into your faith and convictions on biblical manhood. We will need to Man Up! about what it means to follow Jesus. To follow Jesus, young adults in this and the next generation—just like the generations before them—will have to learn how to discipline themselves to a higher calling. Manning up to that calling will determine our future.

The thousands of private boaters who responded to the call of a Coast Guardsman to help evacuate the victims and scared citizens of the 911 disaster could have stayed safely in port or on shore. There would be little risk involved taking that position. But brave people took to their boats, whatever the size and equipment, and helped save their fellow citizens.

So, it is with each one of us. Young, middle aged, or seniors, let's step up and man-up to the challenge before us to rescue those who don't know Jesus to the safety of His presence. And for those Christians sitting on the shoreline of life in comfort, I encourage you to get involved with mentoring young men so that they might be better equipped and enabled to face the challenges of a changing world.

With the power of the Holy Spirit and some fortitude to face the future, we stand our post and do a good job for our Master Teacher. There will be tests, trials, and many unresolved problems, but we will stand fast and not be fearful. We will fight the good fight, for at the end of our journey we, like Jesus, desire to hear those coveted words, "Well done, good and faithful servant; you were faithful over a few things, I will make you ruler over many things. Enter into the joy of your Lord." (Matt. 25:21)

To do this we need to align ourselves with like-minded men. The local church is the obvious place for a Christian man to find the leadership, accountability, encouragement, and resources to equip himself with the tools and spirit he needs to fight the good fight in a chaotic culture. Unfortunately, in most churches around the world, vibrant and dynamic men's ministry programs are just an illusion. At best, most men's ministry programs I've seen become a once-a-month burnt pancake breakfast with a speaker like what you'd find at a secular service club. That doesn't cut it guys!

The New Promise Keepers has launched a major program to assist local churches with the most dynamic and innovative resources that can help equip, train, and guide local fellowships to be an inspiration to their men while reaching out to the unsaved in their communities. Guys—we need each other! Grab on to all the new practical resources, programs, and tools available now through Promise Keepers to help grow your personal and corporate ministries. Visit our new website at www.promisekeepers.org. We are here to assist you and your church.

DISCUSSION QUESTIONS:

1. What are your priorities and plans for retirement? How do those plans and priorities compare with Jesus' command to "Go therefore and make disciples of all the nations" (Matt. 28:19)?

2. What things are you finding within your church that seem divisive or hindering to an effective outreach and discipleship program? What needs to be done to remove such divisive elements?

3. What ideas do you have to help your church and men's group be more intentional about developing a culture of Spiritual Mentoring? Set up a time to speak with your pastor about these ideas.

4. Ponder this thought: *We focus on making a living instead of making time for a life.* Identify a man you can help mentor/disciple and start meeting together. Follow the guidelines we've provided in this book.

EPILOGUE

As a man we will all face many challenges brilliantly disguised as opportunities to grow in our maturity and faith.

Endure hardship as discipline; God is treating you as his children. Therefore, strengthen your feeble arms and weak knees.

– Hebrews 12:7, 12

English author William Wordsworth stated: "The childhood of today is the manhood of tomorrow." Remember, it takes a man to show a man how to be a man. Let's mentor those young people God places in our lives.

A nation or civilization that continues to produce soft-minded men
purchases its own spiritual death on the installment plan.
— Dr. Martin Luther King

In the past nearly forty years of ministry and interaction with men all over the world, I've seen a steady decline and understanding of manhood. I regularly meet with men who feel defeated, frustrated, and confused about their role in a world filled with attacks on the fundamental facets defined by God Almighty about the distinction and roles between the sexes.

The Progressive Movement is redefining the patriarchal society to a feminist agenda. Families disintegrate before children are raised because they lack the protective environment that is inherent with role of a strong father. Unless there is a revolutionary change in our culture, young boys will continue to flounder.

Psychologist Michael Gurian states it well as he summarizes his book *Saving our Sons:*

> *Our boys can help us become the revolutionaries they need us*
> *to be because, when this book ends, you can lift your eyes from*
> *its pages and find males around you. You can look at every boy*
> *and man you know; study his eyes and shoulders, hands and*
> *feet, clothes and masks, listen to his words and silences. Watch*
> *him, observe him, be silent with him, feel his energy, enjoy his*
> *grace, and when the time is right, talk with him about boyhood*
> *and manhood. Ask him how he wants to measure himself, what*

legacy he hopes to leave, how he wants to love his family, spouse, friends, children, and himself...Boys who are loved well give love in ways no civilization can fully measure.[54]

Manhood is not set solely in the masculine norms or a male container but etched into his very soul before birth by a loving Creator. God has great plans for all of us to enter into intimate fellowship with Him and others so that we can live a life of significance and honor. As a man we will all face many challenges brilliantly disguised as opportunities to grow in our maturity and faith. It is through our failures and victories we find the depth of our spirit and fiber so we can meet the Goliath's of our life with the same great faith as the boy David.

The harmony found in a home is largely set by a godly man's leadership. The woman is created to receive, respond, and resonate with their husband's leadership. Therefore, how a husband directs and conducts his home will determine the type of environment that honors our Lord.

The problems in our culture cannot be solved by more government. The problems need to be seen and embraced by the church and responsible Christians who will worry less about crossing the sea to help others but will cross the street to love a single-parent child or a young boy struggling with addictive behaviors.

We need to change the mindset of the church to be a community full of god-fearing, loving, honest men who seek ways to disciple lost souls so they can fully engage with a loving God who is full of mercy, grace, and forgiveness.

In the gospel, Jesus restores our vision of manhood. His life, death, and resurrection show us how restored relationships work. Let's reach out to others for reconciliation, peace, and restoration of our manhood. With God's grace and power, we can and will finish well and strong while reaching a helping hand out to those who are struggling to man up.

E. Stanley Jones was a great man of faith who among many things was a missionary to India. On one trip to this exotic country a friend took him to an amazing sculpture of Christ. The figure of Christ had his arms spread wide with His head bowed down. The only way Stanley could get the full impact of the expression on the Savior's face was to get on his knees and look up into the humble face of the Suffering Servant.

The only way a man can truly humble himself to receive all the instruction and blessings our Lord can provide is for us to bend a knee and prayerfully look into the face of a loving God for wisdom, guidance, and support. His Word and life will teach us how to *Act Like Men,* to Be Strong, and to Man Up! And as we Man Up! let us bring other men with us as we disciple and mentor them.

The local church should be a support to those desiring to grow in their faith. Promise Keepers has many new resources and materials to assist churches, small groups, and individuals with discipleship. Contact us at *www.promisekeepers.org*

GOD'S GAME PLAN FOR LIFE

A mature leader develops a good plan before jumping into a situation. This is paramount to being successful. In a similar manner our heavenly Father wants each of us to be spiritually connected, so He developed a plan for our salvation. He designed man to be linked with Him through His great creation—but Adam and Eve thought they had a better idea.

Then God utilized great patriarchs like Moses and Joshua to present His plan to His chosen people (the Jews). Then He used great kings, priests, judges, and prophets, only to be saddened with the condition of man's prideful spirit and sin filled heart. So how does our Great Guide, God Almighty, get our attention? He sends in the best atoning gifts and the most important sacrifice of all time—Jesus Christ.

The Romans Road lays out God's plan for salvation through a series of Bible verses from the book of Romans. These verses form an easy-to-follow explanation of the message of salvation.

The Roman Road clearly defines:

1. Who needs salvation?

2. Why we need salvation

3. How God provides salvation

4. How we receive salvation

5. The results of salvation

THE ROMAN ROAD TO SALVATION

Everyone needs salvation because we have all sinned.
As it is written: "There is none righteous, no, not one; there is none
who understands; there is none who seeks after God. They have
all turned aside; they have together become unprofitable; there is
none who does good, no, not even one." . . . All have sinned and
fall short of the glory of God. (Rom. 3:10–12, 23)

The price (or consequence) of sin is death.
For the wages of sin is death, but the gift of God is eternal life in
Christ Jesus our Lord. (Rom. 6:23)

Jesus Christ died for our sins. He paid the price for our death.
"But God demonstrates His own love toward us, in that while we
were still sinners, Christ died for us." (Rom. 5:8)

We receive salvation and eternal life through faith in Jesus Christ.

"That if you confess with your mouth the Lord Jesus and believe in your heart that God has raised Him from the dead, you will be saved. For with the heart one believes unto righteousness, and with the mouth confession is made unto salvation. For 'whoever calls on the name of the Lord shall be saved.'" (Rom. 10:9–10, 13)

Salvation through Jesus Christ brings us into a relationship of peace with God.

"Therefore, having been justified by faith, we have peace with God through our Lord Jesus Christ." (Rom. 5:1)

"There is therefore now no condemnation to those who are in Christ Jesus." (Rom. 8:1)

"For I am persuaded that neither death nor life, nor angels nor principalities nor powers, nor things present nor things to come, nor height nor depth, nor any other created thing, shall be able to separate us from the love of God which is in Christ Jesus our Lord." (Rom. 8:38–39)

RESPONDING TO THE ROMANS ROAD

If you believe the Scriptures in Romans lead to the path of truth, you can respond by receiving God's gift of salvation today. Here's how:

1. Admit you are a sinner.
2. Understand that as a sinner, you deserve death.

3. Believe Jesus Christ died on the cross to save you from sin and death. Believe that He conquered death itself when He rose from the grave.

4. Repent by turning from your old life of sin to a new life in Christ.

5. Receive, through faith in Jesus Christ, His free gift of salvation.

Additional Resources

For additional resources or assistance, please e-mail Men's Ministry Catalyst at *www.mensministrycatalyst.org.*

ABOUT THE AUTHOR

 **Jim Grassi, D.Min** is an award-winning author, communicator, outdoorsman, pastor, radio show host, and former television co-host. He has presented hundreds of messages and programs around the world that help equip people to fulfill the Great Commission (Matt. 28). He brings a sense of challenge, wisdom, excitement, and humor to his presentations, as he connects with people of various cultures and backgrounds. Through his multimedia outreach ministry, he encourages participants toward a greater understanding and appreciation of evangelism, discipleship, and creating vibrant men's ministries. His practical approach to teaching biblical truth has captivated audiences around the world.

Jim Grassi is the founder and president of the culturally strategic Men's Ministry Catalyst, an organization he incorporated in 1981. He is now working alongside the leaders at Promise Keepers to help relaunch a global ministry in hopes of producing a major revival.

Grassi is also the recognized author of several books, including *The Ultimate Fishing Challenge, Heaven on Earth, In Pursuit of the Prize, The*

Ultimate Hunt, A Study Guide of Israel, The Ultimate Men's Ministry Encyclopedia, Crunch Time, Crunch Time in the Red Zone, Wading Through the Chaos, Guts, Grace, and Glory—A Football Devotional, The Spiritual Mentor, Building a Ministry of Spiritual Mentoring, More Than a Fisherman, and *Finishing Well—Finishing Strong.* Jim has also written numerous magazine articles, booklets, and tracts. His popular booklet series on men's issues is utilized in many churches and Christian counseling centers.

Dr. Grassi has appeared on many radio and television programs including *Hour of Power, The 700 Club, The Carol Lawrence Show,* Cornerstone Television, Southern Baptist Television—*Cope,* Chicago Television 38, *The Dick Staub Show, Getting Together, In-Fisherman, Fishing Tales, Jimmy Houston Outdoors, Home Life, Focus on the Family, FOX Sports, and CSN.* He is the host of a weekly men's radio program called *Man Up!*

Dr. Grassi was born and reared in the San Francisco Bay area. He and his wife Louise have two grown sons who are serving God as pastors. Known for his evangelistic heart, Grassi teaches people from a background of an outdoorsman, public administrator, Hall of Fame fisherman, college professor, businessman, community leader, and pastor. He has served in the capacity of a chaplain with the San Francisco 49ers, the Oakland Raiders, Hurricane Katrina relief efforts, and local police and fire departments. His life experiences, study of discipleship, and work with hundreds of churches has given him a unique perspective on helping men to know God and make Him known.

ENDNOTES

1   Susanne Babble, PhD, MFT, "Trauma: Childhood Sexual Abuse," *Psychology Today*, March 12, 2013, https://www.psychologytoday.com/us/blog/somatic-psychology/201303/trauma-childhood-sexual-abuse.

2   www.rainn.org/statistics/victims-sexual-violence.

3   Tony Evans, *Kingdom Man: Every Man's Destiny, Every Women's Dream* (Carol Stream, IL: Tyndale House Publishers, 2012), p.2.

4   Eric Mason, *Manhood Restored: How the Gospel Makes Men Whole* (Nashville, TN: B&H Publishing Group, 2013), p.11.

5   Ibid.

6   Richard Hise, *The War Against Men* (Oakland, OR.: Red Anvil, Press, 2004).

7   "Is Eco-Friendly Unmanly? The Green-Feminine Stereotype and Its Effect on Sustainable Consumption?" *Journal of Consumer Research*, Volume 43, Issue 4, December 2016, Pages 567–582, https://doi.org/10.1093/jcr/ucw044.

8   Richard Hise, p.151.

9   Ibid, p.41.

10   Matthew Henry , *Matthew Henry's Commentary on the Whole Bible: Complete and Unabridged in One Volume* (p. 2278).

11   Ibid.

12   Ibid.

13   A. C. Thiselton, *The First Epistle to the Corinthians: a Commentary on the Greek Text* (Grand Rapids, MI: W.B. Eerdmans, 2000). p. 1336.

14   W. H. Green, "Christian Manliness." In *Princeton Sermons* (New York, NY: Fleming H. Revell Company. 1893), pp. 235–246.

15   MacDonald, James, *Act Like Men*. Nashville, TN: LifeWay Resources, 2017 pg. 69.

16   *Church for Men*, www.churchformen.com/allmen.php, October 10, 2006.

17   *UK Christian Handbook online*, www.ukchristianhandbook.org.uk, pg.20, June 2002.

18   *Church for Men*.

19   "California Gov. Newsom: toxic masculinity, xenophobia will lead GOP to become a third party," *The Blaze*, June 24, 2019. *https://www.theblaze.com/california-gov-gavin-newsome-toxic*.

20   Tucker Carlson, *Ship of Fools* (New York, NY, Free Press, 2018), pgs. 202-203.

21   "U.S. Congregational Life Survey–Key Findings," *U.S. Congregations*, October 29, 2003, www.uscongregatioions.org/key.htm.

22   *UK Christian Handbook online*.

23   Taken from messages preached by Pastor Phillip DeCourcy.

24   Pastor Philip Decourcy, "Man Up!" Message delivered on July 14, 2019 at Kindred Community Church in Anaheim, California.

25   Hanna Rosin, *The End of men and the Rise of Women* (New York, NY: Penguin Group, 2012).

26   Michael Gurian, *Saving our Sons* (Spokane, WA: Gurian Institute Press. 2017), pg. 9.

27   W.A. Elwell & P.W. Comfort *Tyndale Bible dictionary* (Wheaton, IL: Tyndale House Publishers 2001), p. 238.

28   "The Extent of Fatherlessness," *Fathers.com*, *http://fathers.com/statistics-and-research/the-extent-of-fatherlessness/*.

29   John Ensor, *Answering the Call* (Colorado Springs, CO: Focus on the Family, 2003), p. 96.

30   Susanne Babble, PhD, MFT, "Trauma: Childhood Sexual Abuse," *Psychology Today*, March 12, 2013, https://www.psychologytoday.com/us/blog/somatic-psychology/201303/trauma-childhood-sexual-abuse.

31   "Victims of Sexual Violence: Statistics," *Rainn*, https://www.rainn.org/statistics/victims-sexual-violence.

32   https://en.wikipedia.org/wiki/Johnny_Weissmuller.

33   Louis L'Amour, *Education of a Wandering Man*.

34   Chuck Stecker, If You Passed Your Baton...Take It Back (Chicago, IL: Seismic Publishing Group), p.79.

35   Ibid, p. 81.

36   Hanna Rosin, "The End of Men—How Women are Taking Control of Everything," *The Atlantic*, July/August 2010 pgs. 60 & 64.

37   Statistic Brain Research Institute, https://www.statisticbrain.com/attention-span-statistics/.

38   Tim Elmore, *Generation iY*, http://generationiy.com/.

39   Zoe Fox, "How Many Teens Are Actually Leaving Facebook?" *Mashable*, January 16, 2014, http://mashable.com/2014/01/16/teens-leaving-facebook/.

40   Tim Elmore, *Generation iY*.

41   Dan Schawbel, "The High School Careers Study," *Millennial Branding*, February 3, 2014, http://millennialbranding.com/2014/high-school-careers-study/.

42   "2011 Cisco Connected World Technology Report," http://www.cisco.com/c/dam/en/us/solutions/enterprise/connected-world-technology-report/2011-CCWTR-Chapter-3-All-Finding.pdf.

43   Tim Elmore, "Six Defining Characteristics of Generation Z, *Growing Leaders, Inc.*, n.d., https://growingleaders.com/blog/six-defining-characteristics-of-generation-z/.

44   Peter Menconi, *The Intergenerational Church* (Litttleton, CO: Mt. Sage Publishing, 2010), p.132.

45   Michael Gurian, *Saving our Sons* (Spokane, WA: Gurian Institute Press, 2017), p.177.

46   Dr. David Jeremiah, "Discipleship Live Learning," *Turning Points Magazine and Devotional*, May 2019, p. 8.

47   David Kinnaman, *You Lost Me* (Grand Rapids, MI: Baker Books, 2011), p.35.

48   Ibid, p.13.

49   Tony Evans, *Kingdom Man: Every Man's Destiny, Every Woman's Dream* (Carol Steam, IL: Tyndale House Publishers, Inc., 2012), p. 30.

50   Ibid, p. 181.

51   James Grassi, *The Spiritual Mentor* (Nashville, TN: Thomas Nelson, 2013), p. xi.

52   Dietrich Bonhoeffer, *The Cost of Discipleship* (New York, NY: Touchstone, 1959), p. 54.

53   George Barna, *Revolution* (Carol Stream, IL: Tyndale House Publishers, Inc., 2005), p. 8.

54   Michael Gurian, p. 262.

MAN CARD COMMITMENT

On the opposite page in this book is a Man Card.

Man Card Definition: *A Promise Keepers Man Card is required proof of biblical manhood in order to become an authentic and respected member of the male community. It can and will be temporarily revoked if privileges as a Man are abused. Uphold the acceptable biblical standards of godly manliness and display your man card proudly. Keep it in your wallet or place it on your mirror to daily remind yourself of your commitment to biblical manhood.*

If you fail in one these areas, then as a man you are accountable to temporarily hold your card until you can correct your behavior in that area. Be accountable to others. Heb. 13:7, Pr.27:17

7 PROMISES OF A PROMISE KEEPER

1. A Promise Keeper is committed to honoring Jesus Christ through worship, prayer and obedience to God's Word in the power of the Holy Spirit.

2. A Promise Keeper is committed to pursuing vital relationships with a few other men, understanding that he needs brothers to help him keep his promises.

3. A Promise Keeper is committed to practicing spiritual, moral, ethical, and sexual purity.

4. A Promise Keeper is committed to building strong marriages and families through love, protection and biblical values.

5. A Promise Keeper is committed to supporting the mission of his church by honoring and praying for his pastor, and by actively giving his time and resources.

6. A Promise Keeper is committed to reaching beyond any racial and denominational barriers to demonstrate the power of biblical unity.

7. A Promise Keeper is committed to influencing his world, being obedient to the Great Commandment (see Mark 12:30-31) and the Great Commission (see Matthew 28:19-20). Mark 12:30-31 Love the Lord your God with all your heart and with all your soul and with all your mind and with all your strength. The second is this: Love your neighbor as yourself. (NIV) Matthew 28:19-20 Therefore go and make disciples of all nations, baptizing them in the name of the Father and of the Son and of the Holy Spirit, and teaching them to obey everything I have commanded you. And surely, I am with you always, to the very end of the age. (NIV)

PROMISE KEEPERS MAN CARD

Cut out the card printed below and fold in half.

A Commitment to God

MAN CARD

PROMISE KEEPERS

FOLD — FOLD

SEVEN PROMISES

HONOR – A Promise Keeper is committed to honoring Jesus Christ

BROTHERHOOD – A Promise Keeper is committed to pursuing vital relationships with a few other men

VIRTUE – A Promise Keeper is committed to practicing spiritual, moral, ethical, and sexual purity

COMMITMENT – A Promise Keeper is committed to building strong marriages and families

CHANGEMAKING – A Promise Keeper understands his authentic identity in Christ and lives a life of integrity

UNITY – A Promise Keeper is committed to reaching beyond any racial and denominational barriers

OBEDIENCE – A Promise Keeper is committed to influencing his world.